Dreamscheme

Irish Studies

DREAMSCHEME

Narrative and Voice in Finnegans Wake

MICHAEL H. BEGNAL

SYRACUSE UNIVERSITY PRESS

MICHAEL H. BEGNAL is Professor of English and Comparative Literature at Pennsylvania State University. He is the author of many books and articles on James Joyce and modern literature, including *Narrator and Character in Finnegans Wake,* and coeditor of *A Conceptual Guide to Finnegans Wake.*

Copyright © 1988 by Syracuse University Press, Syracuse, New York 13244-5160
All Rights Reserved
First published 1988

First Edition

94 93 92 91 90 89 88   6 5 4 3 2 1

The paper used in this publication meets the minimum requirements of American National Standard for Information Sciences—Permanence of Paper for Printed Library Materials, ANSI Z39.48-1984. ∞

Library of Congress Cataloging-in-Publication Data

Begnal, Michael H., 1939–
    Dreamscheme : narrative and voice in Finnegans
wake.
    (Irish studies)
    Bibliography: p.
    Includes index.
    1. Joyce, James, 1882–1941. Finnegans wake.
I. Title. II. Series: Irish studies (Syracuse, N.Y.)
PR6019.09F5535 1987   823'.912   87-26690
ISBN 0-8156-2426-3 (alk. paper)

Manufactured in the United States of America

For
Kate Joan Kilmartin Begnal
(who gave me my first copy of Ulysses)
and
Cynthia Marion Finch Begnal
(who gave me inspiration)

IRISH STUDIES

Irish Studies presents a wide range of books interpreting important aspects of Irish life and culture to scholarly and general audiences. The richness and complexity of the Irish experience, past and present, deserves broad understanding and careful analysis. For this reason an important purpose of the series is to offer a forum to scholars interested in Ireland, its history, and culture. Irish literature is a special concern in the series, but works from the perspectives of the fine arts, history, and the social sciences are also welcome, as are studies which take multidisciplinary approaches.

Irish Studies is a continuing project of Syracuse University Press and is under the general editorship of Richard Fallis, associate professor of English at Syracuse University.

Either one does not dream at all, or he dreams in an interesting manner. One must learn to be awake in the same fashion—either not at all, or in an interesting manner.

—*Friedrich Nietzsche*

Contents

Acknowledgments

Permission has been granted to quote from *Finnegans Wake* by James Joyce. Copyright 1939 by James Joyce. Copyright renewed (c) 1967 by George Joyce and Lucia Joyce. Reprinted by permission of Viking Penguin Inc. And by The Society of Authors as the literary representative of the Estate of James Joyce. Quotes are drawn from James Joyce, *Finnegans Wake* (New York: Viking Press, 1964), and are included in the text, as are quotes from James Joyce, *Ulysses* (New York: Random House, 1986).

Introduction

James Joyce was never at a loss when it came to offering descriptions of what *Finnegans Wake* is all about—the only problem is deciphering the pronouncements. At one moment, he cautioned that "you must not think it is a silly story about the mouse and the grapes. No, it's a wheel, I tell the world. *And* it's all *square*."[1] He once said that writing the novel was like tunneling through a mountain from both sides at once, and another time he recalled a dream of creation: "I was looking at a Turk seated in a bazaar. He had a framework on his knees and on one side he had a jumble of all shades of red and yellow skeins and on the other a jumble of greens and blues of all shades. He was picking from right and left very calmly and weaving away. It is evidently a split rainbow and also Parts I and III."[2] However we may evaluate these Joycean teasers, and whether or not they provide the reader with any relief, it seems clear that Joyce felt that the riddle could be solved through a resolution of opposites, through a fusion of seemingly disparate elements. "It is true that I have been thinking and thinking how and how and how can I and can it—all about the fusion of two parts of the book—while my one bedazzled eye searched the sea like Cain—Shem—Tristan—Patrick from his lighthouse in Boulogne."[3] The problem for him and for us is in putting things together.

In a paradoxical way, just as Joyce protected his secrets and posed his riddles, on the one hand, to keep the scholars guessing for one hundred years, he also went out of his way behind the scenes to encourage the reader and to keep the questing process going. He leaked his plan for *Ulysses* and pretended that it was an accident, and he dropped hints about the title of *Finnegans Wake* until his friends finally guessed it. In a typical comment to Harriet Shaw Weaver, he confided, "The book really has no beginning or end. (Trade secret, registered at Stationers Hall.)."⁴ Like Anna Livia, he has always wanted to be understood. In the years since the *Wake*'s publication in 1939, much valuable spadework has been done to uncover the book's basic form and its themes, though recently, unfortunately, several contemporary critical perspectives, such as structuralism, post-structuralism, and deconstruction seem to have taken us further and further away from the text itself. We need to return to what Joyce actually wrote. If we might agree that the exact meanings of the Joycean statements above mentioned are nothing if not elusive, we might be even more puzzled by some of the recent conjectures emanating from some of the French commentators like Jacques Derrida.⁵

Arguably, *Finnegans Wake* is the most experimental work attempted in prose fiction, and it will not yield to examination easily, but it need not remain a complete enigma. Though the book does not offer a conventional narrative, elements of a plot do continue to drift to the surface. Granted, nothing very much of a physical nature will happen, but as Ivy Compton-Burnett commented, "Real life seems to have no plots."⁶ The *Wake*'s narrative proceeds vertically, rather than horizontally, as one separate incident after another is piled upon what has gone before. The reader must swivel backward and forward and around like the Joycean lighthouse. By concentrating upon these individual incidents, by locating them and analyzing them carefully, we can begin to understand what Joyce is doing with plot and narrative. There are delineated characters immersed in specific situations, whether they be Shem and Shaun, the Mookse and the Gripes, or Burrus and Caseous, and language, not at all simply gesture in Joyce's hands, can help us to identify them. The critical need, then, is for the reader to penetrate into the text, to become accustomed to the various dialects of this night language, while remembering that this is a very funny book. Walt Whitman, in "The Sleepers," might almost be speaking for the reader when he says: "I sleep close with the other sleepers, each in turn; / I dream in my dreams all the dreams of the other dreamers, / And I become the other dreamers."

Whether or not there is a single dreamer in *Finnegans Wake,* and I am fairly convinced that there is not, it is clear that there is an abundance of voices to be heard in this Wakean night. Their cadences and their thematic concerns will sooner or later give them away, if the reader looks and listens closely enough. Though individual scenes and situations are often set up and structured by an unnamed narrational voice, this stylistic entity cannot ever exert total authority over what has once been set in motion. There is no controlling consciousness to which the character voices can be subordinated, so that occasionally they can take off on their own to discuss whatever it is they wish. It has often been written that one salient characteristic of these Earwicker speakers is their obsessive desire to hide the centers of their respective psyches from their fellows and from the reader, but instead it appears that in their long and meandering monologues, in their staccato question-and-answer sessions, they almost tell us more than we need or want to know. And they are not so difficult to discover behind their narrational masks, since they always make their appearances in virtually the same combinations—brother warring against brother when Shem and Shaun are on the stage, and the suitor looking for a wife when the turns come for Anna Livia and Humphrey Chimpden Earwicker.[7] Unfailingly, when Issy comes forward at all, she will adopt the role of the supporting actress.

One of the major contributions of *Finnegans Wake* to the development of narrational technique is Joyce's experimentation with the very idea of plot itself. At the same time, however, it should be noted that Joyce is very much the traditionalist when it comes to the ways in which he will manipulate plot and character. Certainly what he does is new, but it builds upon what has been written in the past and upon what he has already established in his previous works of fiction. In some ways the overlapping fables in the *Wake* are a more complex reflection of the multiple views of paralysis which were offered in *Dubliners,* while the conception of a narrative rooted in psychological perception, rather than physical action, should be familiar from the growth of Stephen's consciousness in *A Portrait of the Artist as a Young Man.* The multiple voices which shift back and forth in the *Wake* recall the many narrational devices in *Ulysses;* with each new chapter comes yet another new point of view, while time and space break free from any conventional boundaries. All such possibilities come together here. The method in *Finnegans Wake* is not random, and by concentrating closely upon the structure and the language of the novel the reader can follow the signposts which lead to Joyce's grand design. Joyce never promised that this would be easy, but the insights, the laughter, and the rewards will more than justify the midnight oil.

1

So This Is Dyoublong?
(13.04)

E ver since portions of *Finnegans Wake,* originally titled *Work
in Progress,* began to appear in *transition,* the overwhelming
question has been: what is it all about? While it is a fact that early
reviewers were hard put to make any sense of the work, and a great
many reacted with anger, frustration, and scorn, it is not quite true
that Joyce's novel met with universal incomprehension. From the
outset, a good number of critics were concerned with discovering a
form beneath the seeming chaos of the surface. Writing in *Experi-
ment* in 1931, Stuart Gilbert noted, "The form . . . may be likened
to a carefully planned and exactly ordered fantasia. . . . For it is the
paradox of this work to be at once fantastic and extremely sym-
metrical; nothing could be further from the super-realist 'free
writing,' yet a reader's first impression is one of confusion, a vivid
welter of ideas and free associations. A baroque superstructure
hides the steel frame beneath."[1] We know that Gilbert often talked
to Joyce about *Ulysses* and *Finnegans Wake,* and this emphasis on
structure and control is buttressed by the comments of another of
Joyce's friends, Frank Budgen:

> It has often been said of Joyce that he was greatly influenced by
> psychoanalysis in the composition of *Ulysses* and *Finnegans
> Wake.* . . . But if it is meant that he adopted the theory and followed
> the practice of psychoanalysis in his work as did the Dadaists and the
> Surrealists, nothing could be farther from the truth. The Joycean
> method of composition and the passively automatic method are two

opposite and opposed poles. . . . Joyce was always impatient or contemptuously silent when it was talked about as both an all-sufficient *Weltanschauung* and a source and law for artistic production. "Why all this fuss and bother about the mystery of the unconscious?" he said to me one evening at the Pfauen Restaurant. "What about the mystery of the conscious? What do they know about that?" One might say that both as man and artist Joyce was exceedingly conscious. Great artificers have to be.[2]

Perhaps, paradoxically, a reader must be active and wide awake to approach the dream landscape of *Finnegans Wake,* to deal with the novelty of Joyce's novel.

One initial question we might now ask, to begin with the ending rather than with the beginning, is whether or not the novel has a conclusion. Much has been made of the *Wake*'s circular structure, of its final suspended sentence which runs back into the first, of its seemingly intentional inability to end. Joyce told Louis Gillet that he selected the last word in this way: "This time, I have found the word which is the most slippery, the least accented, the weakest word in English, a word which is not even a word, which is scarcely sounded between the teeth, a breath, a nothing, the article *the*."[3] Yet, at the same time, the novel does seem to be trying to stop. Though the final word is indeed the noncommital "the" (628.16), and the Anna Livia voice has just acknowledged, "I read in Tobe-continued's tale" (626.18), she still attempts to finish. She recognizes her passing out ("O bitter ending!" [627.35]), and she wishes to be free of the bustling rush of words ("End here" [628.13]), but the language carries her along for three more lines before it will release her. It is almost as if Anna Livia is torn between the need for closure and the need to get as much as possible into the speech before it is too late, much as Molly Bloom crammed detail upon detail, association upon association, before her triumphant "yes":

"and the sea the sea crimson sometimes like fire and the glorious sunsets and the figtrees in the Alameda gardens yes and all the queer little streets and pink and blue and yellow houses and the rosegardens and the jessamine and geraniums and cactuses and

Gibraltar as a girl where I was a Flower of the mountain yes"
(*Ulysses,* 643.1598).

But of course Joyce has complicated or avoided his endings
many times before. The first sentence of *Dubliners,* "There was no
hope for him this time," sounds like it might fittingly be the last,
and our concluding view of Gabriel Conroy leaves him staring out
of a hotel window, with no idea who he is or what he might do
next. The conclusion of *A Portrait of the Artist* is actually another
beginning, since Stephen Dedalus seems to be off for Paris and a
new life, and such open-endedness is reflected in later speculations
as to whether Bloom will receive his often-discussed breakfast in
bed from a chastened or astonished Molly. Earlier in *Ulysses,* Joyce
had played with conceptions of beginnings and endings in the
Sirens chapter. After an introductory page and a half of musical
overture, we have an ending ("Done"), and a new beginning
("Begin!" [*Ulysses,* 211.63]). This is picked up on the chapter's last
page where Robert Emmet's speech on the gallows strains to
unfold but is held back, suspended, by Bloom's attack of gas until
another "done" resounds: "I'm sure it's the burgund. Yes. One,
two. *Let my epitaph be.* Kraaaaaa. *Written. I have.* Pprrpffrrppffff.
Done" (*Ulysses,* 239.1290). To echo what John Donne said about
his own relationship with God, it seems that when Joyce hast done,
he hast not done.

Examining the conventions of narrative fiction, Frank Kermode
has observed that "one of the most powerful of the local and
provincial restrictions is that a novel must *end,* or pretend to; or
else score a point, by disappointing the expectation that it will do
so. There must be *closure* or at least an allusion to it. The tabu
sacralizes closure; it suggests that to give away the solution that
comes at the end is to give away all, so intense is the hermeneutic
specialisation."[4] In *Finnegans Wake* there are many apparent, immediate endings to specific incidents or episodes, such as the fables
of the Prankquean, or Buckley and the Russian General, or the
Ondt and the Gracehoper. Book I, chapter 6 consists of a series of
twelve questions and twelve apparently neat answers, but the problem is that the answers do not really fit the questions, so that in

form we have closure, but in essence we do not. Several of the chapters end with a movement into deeper sleep: I.3, "Rain. When we sleep. Drops. But wait until our sleeping. Drain. Sdops" (74.18); I.8, "Beside the rivering waters of, hitherandthithering waters of. Night!" (216.04); II.1, "Ha he hi ho hu. Mummum" (259.09); III.2, "morroweth whereon every past shall full fost sleep. Amain" (473.24). But a speaker is always awake once again in the following chapter. Several of the chapters appear to end like the closing of a letter: I.5, "Shem the Penman" (125.23); II.2, "from jake, jack and little sousoucie (the babes that mean too)" (308.23); III.3, "Mattaha! Marahah! Luahah! Joahanahanahana!" (554.10). But no definitive text of this letter is ever established, and version after version keeps popping up out of the midden heap. A decisive conclusion can never be achieved, perhaps because this is the psychological nature of reality.

Continuing, Kermode takes a look at contemporary criticism: "I am reminded of a lucid observation made by Barthes some years ago, before he developed his later method of analysis. 'A work of literature,' he said then, 'or at least of the kind that is normally considered by the critics (and this itself may be a possible definition of "good" literature) is neither ever quite meaningless (mysterious or "inspired") nor ever quite clear; it is, so to speak, *suspended* meaning; it offers itself to the reader as a declared system of significance, but as a signified object it eludes his grasp.' "[5] In some ways, this statement could be applied to Joyce's novel, but with a twist. *Finnegans Wake* has suspended closure, on its surface appearance, but it does not have suspended meaning. In actuality, of course, the book does end on its final page, since the reader does not immediately turn back to the first page and begin all over again.

One aspect of the *Wake*'s "declared system of significance" is that its inability to end reflects the inability of consciousness and existence to end in an archetypal sense. Hugh Kenner's description of *Ulysses* might have bearing here as well: "Joyce's aesthetic of delay, producing the simplest facts by parallax, one element now, one later, and leaving large orders of fact to be assembled late or another time or never, in solving the problem of novels that go flat after we know 'how it comes out' also provides what fiction has never before really provided, an experience comparable to that of experiencing the haphazardly evidential quality of life; and, moreover, what art is supposed to offer that life cannot, a permanence to be revisited at will but not exhausted."[6] (The structure of this gargantuan sentence demonstrates its point.)

When a reader is finished with the novel, he or she has absorbed a vast amount of material, an almost endless stream of "unfacts," but certainly this reader does not need to know any more. The essential qualities of male and female, of youth and age, have been thoroughly set out before us, and thus the text sets up a flow or a thrust backward to what has come before, as will be examined later in more detail. What lies behind the surface of apparently random detail leads us ultimately toward a certain underlying certainty.

Yet, this "certainty" should be somewhat qualified. Following Barthes's dichotomy, we should first agree that the *Wake* is neither "mysterious" nor "inspired" in his sense (though, in another sense it is), and William T. Noon finds that "the alert reader soon perceives that the illusion which Joyce is striving to create is not the problem of incoherent dreaming but of most consciously controlled and patterned comic art."[7] Indeed, at the same time, the work will not roll over thematically and play dead. It will never be completely clear, as no work of art ever is, and the critical problem remains the discovery of imbedded patterns. It will not do to veer to the opposite pole and treat the text as if it were a crossword puzzle.[8] If the novel demonstrates any certainty, it is that existence—like history, as Stephen Dedalus learned—will not yield its secrets to specific, logical questioning. The first question the reader is asked is, "But was iz?" (4.14), and the last question is, "is there one who understands me?" (627.15). Between the two lies the body of *Finnegans Wake,* its totality incorporating the fusion of "was" and "is" and providing a hesitant "yes" to Anna Livia's query. The novel is not a detective story, but the reader must steer a reasonable course between immediate detail and archetypal inclusiveness. Frank Budgen recalls, "August Suter told me that when Tuohy was painting Joyce's portrait he said something about the artist's soul. 'Get the artist's soul out of your mind,' said Joyce, 'and see that you paint my tie properly.' "9

To speculate about questions is also, by implication, to inquire about who is asking them. Just what is the basic principle of the narration? Bombarded for years by explicatory letters from Joyce himself, Harriet Shaw Weaver has this to say: "The ascription of the whole thing to a dream of HCE seems to me nonsensical. My view is that Mr. Joyce did not intend the book to be looked upon as the dream of any one character, but that he regarded the dream form with its shiftings and changes and chances as a convenient device, allowing the freest scope to introduce any material he wished—and suited to a night-piece."10 Though no one has yet come up with a satisfactory principle for *Wake* telling, there have been several insightful comments about *Ulysses.* Hugh Kenner has identified the presence of what he calls the Arranger standing behind the variations of narrative perspective,11 and had earlier offered the Uncle Charles Principle for explaining the interplay between the describer and the thing described12 (which will be discussed later in this study). Moving ahead, Shari and Bernard Benstock, noting some of the difficulties with Kenner's position, have formulated the Benstock Principle: "*Fictional texts that exploit free indirect speech* [the narrational mode most common to *Ulysses*] *establish the contextual supremacy of subject matter, which influences the direction, tone, pace, point of view, and method of narration.*"13

This is quite a useful observation, since it seems that perhaps half of the time, this is true as well for *Finnegans Wake,* though again, perhaps half of the time it is not. In a situation such as that in I.2, where an apparently impersonal narrator, not to be definitely named, is discussing the genealogy of Humphrey Chimpden Earwicker, the tone and style of the voice become almost those of a pleasant, informed, slightly boring researcher. "Concerning the genesis of Harold or Humphrey Chimpden's occupational agnomen . . . and discarding once for all those theories from older sources which would link him back with such pivotal ancestors as the Glues, the Gravys, the Northeasts, the Ankers and the Earwickers of Sidlesham in the Hundred of Manhood or proclaim him offsprout of vikings who had founded wapentake and seddled hem in Herrick or Eric, the best authenticated version, the Dumlat . . . has it that it was this way" (30.02). "Agnomen" and "offsprout" are words that a scholar of this sort would in all likelihood use, and the subject is dictating the way in which it will be described. So too, when the beautiful Isolde is described by a narrator in II.4, who might be the first cousin of the speaker in Cyclops, the language takes on a contemporary slang and crudity: "There was this, wellyoumaycallher, a strapping modern old ancient Irish prissces, so and so hands high, such and such paddock weight, in her madapolam smock, nothing under her hat but red hair and solid ivory (now you know it's true in your hardup hearts!) and a firstclass pair of bedroom eyes, of most unhomy blue" (396.06). The subject is the debasement in the present of what might be called the ideal of courtly love, and the Benstock Principle works well in instances such as these.

A very large portion of the *Wake* narrative, however, is presented to us from the point of view and in the voice of a specific, or at least recognizable, character. In these sections or portions of the discourse, it almost invariably holds true that, once we can identify the voice and the style, the source of a particular speech, we can anticipate what the subject matter will be. For if, as we shall see, the character voices have something of a narrow range of subjects about which they seem compelled to speak, it will not always be quite correct to state that "the reader must supply for himself the principles that govern the contextual setting of action in the text, must divine for himself the relationship that exists between the subject as narrated and the process by which it is narrated."[14] Once we know that Shaun incessantly commingles food, religion, and sex, always assumes a dictatorial tone, and can be discovered as the speaker as he is in III.2, we virtually expect him to say things such as, "Never miss your lost somewhere mass for the couple in Myles you butrose to brideworship. Never hate mere pork which is bad for your knife of a good friday. Never let a hog of the howth trample underfoot your linen of killiney" (433.10). We can expect Issy, with her flirtatious tone and babytalk, to carry on with her simpering thoughts of romance: Did you really never in all our cantalang lives speak clothse to a girl's before? No! Not even to the charmermaid? How marfellows!" (148.22). The Benstocks are rightly cautious of ascribing intentions and human characteristics to a narrative voice or to a narrator, but oftentimes the *Wake* characters confront the reader directly, speak knowingly to a reader who they know is reading and listening.

One of the most problematic aspects of *Wake* narration is the narrative voices which cannot be precisely identified, the voices which set a scene or tell a story in accents which are not immediately locatable. The phenomenon of narrative styles which, especially in the second half of *Ulysses,* proliferate in leaps and bounds is at work in a different way throughout the whole of *Finnegans Wake.* What Harriet Shaw Weaver called "shiftings and changes and chances" applies specifically to these voices, though they seem to have a common characteristic. Like the Earwicker family voices, they always snap the audience to attention by addressing the reader, by pulling him or her into the action of whatever is at hand. Thus, our escort through the Museyroom says, "Phew! What a warm time we were in there but how keling is here the airabouts!" (10.24), or the commentator at the trial of Festy King, "And so it all ended. Artha kama dharma moksa. Ask Kavya for the kay" (93.22). Sometimes these speakers have noticeable accents, and sometimes they do not, but in *Finnegans Wake* it becomes clear that multiplicity of voice is Joyce's substitute for the multiplicity of styles he employed in *Ulysses.* While we might suspect that each of these voices is a variation or a masked version of a member of the Earwicker chorus, this is not always so easy to prove. It is probably a good guess that the stern professor who tells the tale of Burrus and Caseous is Shaun, given his already mentioned predilections: "We now romp through a period of pure lyricism of shamebred music (technologically, let me say, the appetising entry of this subject on a fool chest of vialds is plumply pudding the carp before doevre hors)" (164.15), with guilt, food, and a swipe at *Chamber Music.* But the narrator of the Norwegian Captain story does not display such obvious identifying marks: "Infernal machinery (serial number: Bullysacre, dig care a dig) having thus passed the buck to billy back from jack (finder the keeper) as the baffling yarn sailed in circles it was now high tide for the reminding pair of snipers to be suitably punished" (320.33). Just as there are tales within tales, there are voices within voices, and they are not all to be approached in exactly the same way. So much of *Finnegans Wake* becomes a dialogue back and forth, that we must do our best to delineate each new speaker.

The overwhelming crux of the *Wake* is undeniably explication. How can we say that there is something of a plot, that we have a reasonable idea of what is going on, if the language is so dense and impenetrable that no two people can ever seem to agree? Admittedly, in a book of this kind there can be no one "right" interpretation, but we can arrive at a ground of "right" or admissible views which can be tolerated or allowed by sticking as closely as we possibly can to the actual text. As Kermode states reasonably, "The pluralities of sense available to *zoon phonanta* [the speaking animal] appear to be indeterminate but nonetheless systematically limited. That suggests that we can have a humanly adequate measure of plurality without abandoning all notions of consensual interpretation."[15] It might be helpful to put four different critical versions of a particular passage up against one another to see just what happens when Wakese meets the light of day. Without attempting to elevate one over another, to say that one is better than another, here are four among several versions of how Earwicker got his name (30.01–31.33) offered by Joseph Campbell and Henry Morton Robinson in 1944, William York Tindall in 1969, Adaline Glasheen in 1977, and Danis Rose and John O'Hanlon in 1982:

> One sultry sabbath afternoon, in pre-fall paradise peace, while the grand old gardener was plowing in the rear of his house, royalty was announced to have halted itself in the course of a foxhunt on the highroad. Forgetful of all save his vassal's plain fealty, Humphrey, or Harold, stumbled out hotface as he was . . . jingling his turnpike keys and bearing aloft a high perch atop of which was a flowerpot fixed with care. His Majesty, instead of inquiring directly why yon causeway was thus potholed, asked to know what flies were being

favored these days for lobster-trapping. . . . Our sailor king smiled beneath his walrus mustaches and turned toward two of his retinue . . . and remarked dilsydulsily: "Holy bones of St. Hubert, how our red brother of Pouring-rainia would audibly fume did he know that we have for surtrusty baliwick a turnpiker who is by turn a pikebailer no seldomer than an earwigger!"[16]

Earwicker got his name from this: One evening while a royal fox-hunt was in progress . . . the king and his cocker spaniels, pausing on the turnpike at the "mobhouse" or pub in Chapelizod, surprise the turnpike-keeper-publican catching earwigs in his garden after the manner of "cabbaging Cincinnatus." Singing "John Peel" (a song that will recur), the king names the gardener "earwigger" on the spot.[17]

On the eve of Chevy Chase, William the Conk . . . out foxhunting . . . with two of his soldiers, stops to drink Adam's ale in Adam's innyard or in the holding of William's vassal Harold . . . who also keeps a turnpike. . . : The turnpike is potholed, and Harold-Humphrey betrayingly carries a pot of earth on a long pole—Finnegan's ever-helping hod. Harold has stolen the earth from the king, his feudal lord, God's earthly representative. The king asks Harold, did he do it to trap lobsters (redcoats)? (The IRA did pothole roads against the Black and Tans.) Harold says virtuously, no, he was catching earwigs. The answer establishes the vassal's loyalty (how?) and enables the Conk to make a witticism about having a trusty turnpiker who is also an earwigger. . . . After the exchange of water and name, humble Humphrey is presumably allowed to hold his bit of earth and is humble no more.[18]

One sunny, sultry sabbath afternoon Humphrey was peacefully (it was before his fall) ploughing up roots in the back garden of his madhouse when it was made known to him by a runner that a royal party had halted from a fox-hunt on the highroad outside. Alert to his obligations, the vassal serf hurried out as he was . . . jingling his turnpike keys and bearing aloft amid the hoisted bayonets of the hunting party a pole with a flower pot on the top. His Majesty, who had stopped behind his spaniels merely to inquire what had caused all the pot-holes in the road, caught sight of Humphrey's rod and . . . asked instead the honest, blunt, hot-faced Saxon before him

what he fancied for bait at the present time. . . . No, your Majesty,
the gardener hastily replied, I was just catching bloody earwigs.[19]

The discernible differences in these four versions can be attribut-
able to areas of emphasis, on the one hand, and a reading or
misreading of the actual text itself, on the other. The first stays close
to the text, quotes and paraphrases; the second tries to be concise
and reduces the narrative to a brief story; the third seems to work
mainly by association, questioning itself as it goes along; the
fourth, like the first, attempts something like a literal narrative.
Though they all agree that a fox hunt originates the action, the
second states that the incident took place at night, which is clearly
contradicted by Joyce's words, and the fourth adds that it was
sunny. What was Harold or Humphrey doing? One says that he
was plowing in his garden, while two and three agree that he was
catching earwigs. Four goes along with one but notices a
madhouse on the premises rather than a pub. None questions why
he might be doing such a thing. One, three, and four agree that the
king was worried about the potholes in the road, and one brings in
the possibility of lobster trapping, which three extends to include
the implied presence of redcoats or the Black and Tans, asserting
further that Humphrey was stealing pots of dirt for some unex-
plained reason. Four finds that the king is simply interested in
fishing. One and three note that Humphrey is carrying a flower pot
on a long pole, but neither comments on this outlandish behavior,
though three notes that he brandishes the pole "betrayingly." Four,
in a footnote, says that this is a common device for trapping
earwigs, but the king mistakes it for a fishing pole.[20]
Despite these demonstrated discrepancies, all four critiques
come together in agreement that the Earwicker family got its name
because its forebearer was associated with an insect, the earwig.
The problem lies not with the core of meaning, but rather with the
level of association which exists above or below the text itself.
Certain details or aspects of the story are ignored either because
they are deemed not very important, or possibly because the com-

mentator has no truly plausible explanation. Fritz Senn and Clive Hart argued the problem of what is a reasonable interpretation of a given *Wake* passage and what is not throughout the pages of *A Wake Newslitter,* and, understandably, nothing was ever finally resolved. But still I would contend that, whatever *Finnegans Wake* is about, it is concerned with stories which are told to the reader from many different points of view, stories which are composed of words—words, strange as many of them are, which can only have so many possible meanings. Thus, in this tale of how Earwicker got his name, we cannot ignore the earwigs, but the IRA and the Black and Tans should probably be ruled out of bounds. This sort of allusion, interesting as it may be, moves us further afield from meaning, rather than pointing directly at the center of the text. The point of this study is not to disallow certain avenues of interpretation, flailing about with a club of critical censure, but instead to locate and describe aspects of narrative technique and threads of narrative itself so that we might arrive at some consensus and estimation of the clean-living giant and his associates who began their careers as earwiggers.

To do so, we must look for some sort of plot by examining specific passages in detail. As John Peale Bishop concluded only a year after the novel's publication, HCE "can be sought on the realistic level, as can every other personage in the book; if he could not be found there we should not be concerned with his history. The common man includes all history; he is what he is because of all heroes and saints. What was, is."[21] True, things are not all so easy as this, but the Joycean reader must look closely at the narrative to discover a trail through the wilderness. Would Stephen Dedalus and Leopold Bloom have considered reading *Finnegans Wake?* (Molly might be astute enough to notice that there is something smutty in this one, as opposed to *Ruby: the Pride of the Ring,* though, o rocks, it is not told in plain words.) Stephen would probably not be very much interested, since he spends the majority of his time reading in the book of himself, with little concern for the contemporary publishing scene. But Bloom might just look for the story, since he knows that all novels must have one, and it might find a place on his bookshelf between Hozier's *History of the Russo-Turkish War* and Allingham's *Laurence Bloomfield in Ireland.* Good references, those. Perhaps, after looking into *Finnegans Wake,* he might see there what he saw reflected in the gilt-bordered mirror above the mantelpiece in his own livingroom: "What composite asymmetrical image in the mirror then attracted his attention? / The image of a solitary (ipsorelative) mutable (aliorelative) man" (*Ulysses,* 581.1348). Solitary, self-contained, changeable, externally oriented, all are adjectives which could be applied in equal measure to Humphrey Chimpden Earwicker and the members of his household.

2

My Drummers Have Tattled
Tall Tales of Me

(545.26)

In an often-quoted comment from a letter to Harriet Shaw Weaver, James Joyce said: "One great part of every human existence is passed in a state which cannot be rendered sensible by the use of wideawake language, cutanddry grammar and goahead plot."[1] Plot or narrative in conventional Western fiction has almost always been "goahead," has almost always been structured around a beginning, a middle, and an end. The opening tag, "once upon a time," alerts the reader to expect sooner or later the satisfying closure of "and they all lived happily (or unhappily) ever after." Obviously, however, with the Modernist fixation upon the conscious and the unconscious, upon association rather than logic, such a neat packaging of experience will no longer do. In *Finnegans Wake,* perhaps the most experimental fiction ever attempted, Joyce takes great pains to undercut the formal expectations of plot and to demonstrate that narrative must be adapted to the mental processes it attempts to represent.

One central characteristic of *Wake* narrative is that it constantly strains against itself, rebels against the forward impulse and turns back to what has gone before.[2] The very first sentence of the work reveals a Liffey River whose current has reversed direction and points back to its source in space and time: "riverrun, past Eve and Adam's, from swerve of shore to bend of bay, brings us by a commodius vicus of recirculation *back* to Howth Castle and Environs" (3.01, emphasis mine). To complete the final sentence of Anna Livia's monologue: "A way a lone a last a loved a long the"

15

(628.15), the reader must return to the initial sentence of the text. The church of Adam and Eve has become Eve and Adam's, and the narration pauses a moment to look at itself from behind. Thus a reader must realign his or her critical perspective and be prepared to read almost from right to left.

The conditioned impulse to look ahead to the next word or to the next sentence for meaning and comprehensibility is consistently frustrated. Like some literary traffic policeman, Joyce insists that we apply the brakes at almost every turn. "(Stoop) if you are abcedminded to this claybook, what curios of signs (please stoop), in this allaphbed!" (18.17). "Here (please to stoop). . . . (O stoop to please)" (19.02). And the exhortations never cease: "Please stoop O to please. Stop. What saying?" (232.18). More often than not, the *Wake* sentence itself is periodic, a labyrinthian collection of phrases, clauses, and parentheses which seems to strive against completion, as if just a little more information will make everything come right for a reader balked and befuddled already.

We arrive at *Wake* meaning through a process of accrual, so that each new element or piece of plot makes sense only as it reminds us of what has gone before and as it restates a basic crux or situation. The repetition of theme or incident necessitates the building of vertical towers of information which require immediate reference back to their analogues. To comprehend the present of the narrative, we must make that "utterly unexpected sinistrogyric return to one peculiar sore point in the past" (120.27), with "sinistrogyric" the key. While spinning contentedly at his or her place in the text, the reader is instructed to turn to the left, to reconsider the pictures which have already been shown. Again: "Shop! Please shop! Shop ado please! O ado please shop!" (560.16). In no matter what order we read them, the words insist on the very same point.

The devices Joyce uses to spike the progression of goahead plot are many, and they range from specific interruptions to the structures of entire chapters and even Books of *Finnegans Wake*. As Shaun excoriates his brother Shem in I.7, he is halted by an interpolated advertisement for a butcher's shop: "Johns is a different butcher's. Next place you are up town pay him a visit. Or better still, come tobuy" (172.05). A few pages later, Shaun's harangue pauses for what seems to be an ad in the newspaper's personals column from a connoisseur of ladies' underwear which is labeled an "ABORTISEMENT": "Jymes wishes to hear from wearers of abandoned female costumes, gratefully received, wadmel jumper, rather full pair of culottes and onthergarmenteries, to start city life together" (181.30). The nameless narrator exercises his editorial prerogative to step in and to manipulate the flow of the text whenever he wishes, and he refuses to allow us to be carried away by the rush of Shaun's vituperation. A paragraph in Latin (185) soon after is food for thought and is certainly the kind of erudite offering which Shaun would not be up for. (Neither are some of Joyce's readers.)

At the end of the chapter the narration is taken out of Shaun's hands altogether, and we are left with the counterstatements of the Shaun-Shem surrogates JUSTIUS and MERCIUS. A smooth progression from beginning to end in the chapter will not be allowed, and instead the reader must put together a jumble of bits and pieces which a backward-looking narrator has carefully arranged. As we will be cautioned later, "down the gullies of the eras we may catch ourselves looking forward to what will in no time be staring you larrikins on the postface in that multimirror megaron of returningties" (582.18).

Joyce repeats this technique of narrator interpolation over and over again. In the Norwegian Captain episode in II.3, the struggle of the Captain and Kersse the Tailor is halted by a weather report on the television set in HCE's pub: "Windth from the nordth. Warmer towards muffinbell, Lull" (324.25). This is followed by a newsflash which momentarily stops the action again: "Giant crash in Aden. . . . Burial of Lifetenant-Groevener Hatchett, R. I. D." (324.36). The dramatic potential of the conflict is consistently undercut throughout the fable by disconcerting narrational comments, asides, cautions, and even a singing group's parodic version of "John Peel": "Chorus: With his coate so graye. And his pounds that he pawned from the burning" (322.14).

In the same chapter, Butt and Taff seek to combine their powers to accomplish the shooting of the Russian General, but they must pause in the middle of their piece for an on-the-scene description of a steeplechase in progress. *"Emancipator, the Creman hunter (Major Hermyn C. Entwhistle) with dramatic effect reproducing the form of famous sires on the scene of the formers triumphs, is showing the eagle's way to Mr Whaytehayte's three buy geldings Homo Made Ink, Bailey Beacon and Ratatuohy"* (342.19). Soon after, the twins must wait again for another news bulletin concerning the splitting of the atom: *"The abnihilisation of the etym by the grisning of the grosning of the grinder of the grunder of the first lord of Hurtreford"* (353.22).

Each of these examples, and there are many more in each episode, serve to throw the text back upon itself. They interrupt narrational continuity, and they cause the reader to jog in place, to jump back to the beginning of a piece and reassess before moving along once again.

The very form of individual chapters demonstrates the resistance to goahead plot. The Lessons chapter, II.2, complicates the problem of reading a text by including "marginalia by the twins, who change sides at halftime, footnotes by the girl (who doesn't)."[3] The physical act of moving one's eyes down the page is impeded by a structure which forces our gaze off the central narrative to the left, to the right, and to the bottom of the page. The questions which pop out of each paragraph are certainly not to be answered in a jiffy, since the reader is too busy switching attention from one part of the text to another: "Who is he? Whose is he? Why is he? How much is he? Which is he? When is he? Where is he?[4] How is he? And what the decans is there about him anyway, the decemt man? Easy, calm your haste!" (261.28). The Shaunian sidenote describes this section as the: "CONSTITUTION OF THE CONSTITUTIONABLE AS CONSTITUTIONAL" (not much help), while Issy's footnote offers: "[4]Bhing, said her burglar's head, soto poce." Shem does not bother to comment at all. Rather than elucidating meaning, in many cases the notes serve only to plunge the reader even deeper into darkness, as the text proceeds to deny its own conventional implications of communication. If we are taken aback by Shem's: "Undante umoroso. M. 50–50" (269.L), we should have been prepared by wrestling with Issy's: "³H' dk' fs' h'p'y./ ⁴Googlaa pluplu" (265.fn.). These are instances where Joyce consciously employs *non sequitur* with misshapen musical terms and perhaps "handkerchiefs halfpenny," to turn us back and redirect our reading to something somewhere else. Wide-awake language has fallen asleep, along with cut-and-dry grammar, and we turn back to firmer ground.

Shari Benstock offers an extremely interesting analysis of this chapter by positing that the text is supplied by Kev and Dolph Porter, the sidenotes by Shem and Shaun from a more mature perspective, and the footnotes by Issy simultaneous with the ongoing action. Though it seems to me that Porter is simply another version of Earwicker, and Kevin and Dolph alter egos of Shaun and Shem, Benstock makes the point that "the notes vary in tone and establish a new narrative that runs both parallel and counter to the 'primary' narrative."[4] She feels that Issy's notes split in two to form a dialogue like that of the washerwomen in the Anna Livia chapter, setting up several levels of narrative which are all going on at the same time. Thus, "these notes play on the extension of authority provided by the scholarly apparatus—offering the illusion of a receding chain of previous and multiple references while also establishing the notational hierarchy out of which arises the dialogue that divides the text against itself."[5] Once again, narrative coils back upon itself and will not adhere to the straight and narrow.

Along with the disconcerting structure of this chapter goes what might be called a disruption of voice, to be discussed in greater detail later. But here four different speakers are vying for our attention, and they do so in radically different ways. Shem, at first on the left, is often boisterous and mercurial—*"Will you carry my can and fight the fairies?"* (268.L)—and his tone does not change when he moves over to the right: "SICK US A SOCK WITH SOME SEDIMENT IN IT FOR THE SAKE OF OUR DARNING WIVES" (300.R). Shaun, as we might expect, remains pedantically professorial whenever he appears. Issy makes jokes: "³Wipe your glosses with what you know" (304.fn.), and she can even lose interest altogether: "⁴I've lost the place, where was I" (307.fn.). Meanwhile, the central narrative continues merrily along with what seems to be an account of the children at their homework. With so many voices talking at us all at once, with such immense variations in tone, it is difficult to proceed without a constant reevaluation of just what it is that we are reading and listening to. Perhaps Joyce might have occasionally recalled an aphorism of Friedrich Nietzsche's from *The Joyful Wisdom*, a volume which was part of Joyce's personal Triestine library: "*Historia abscondita*—Every great man has a power which operates backward; all history is again placed on the scales on his account, and a thousand secrets of the past crawl out of their lurking places—into his sunlight."⁶ It is debatable how much sunlight appears in this Wakean night, but the emphasis on verticality and on looking backward underscores recurring leitmotiv as the key to comprehending plot and theme in the novel.

It is a commonplace to say that *Finnegans Wake* transcends conventional space and time, but Joyce is offering a new way of reading history as well as a text. "History as her is harped" (486.06), "Storiella as she is syung" (267.17), have, in Joyce's view, led us astray. The problem with the accepted or Christan way of viewing history is that it is linear and logical, and ultimately it is pessimistic. Whether we begin our counting from the Garden of Eden or from the "big bang," time and history move linearly point by point toward the inevitable Last Judgment or the dying of the Sun. Each event in time proceeds from what has gone before, and each event looks forward to the next. Out of nothingness, we are moving along to nothingness.

In form, *Finnegans Wake* rejects this negativity by becoming a circle in which plot and character can never end (unless the reader throws down the book in frustration), and meaning is located not in the proximity of one event to the next, but rather in the essential resemblances which one event can have to another, no matter how widely separated by space and time. Thus, we wrestle with the significance of the Norwegian Captain's tale by turning, at one and the same time, back to the Museyroom and ahead to the Ondt and the Gracehoper. Actually, after completing the circle of the novel's narrative for the first time, distinctions of forward and back no longer exist, and the reader is freed to pile archetype upon archetype, similarity upon similarity, as the second reading begins.

The constant impediments to goahead plot are insistent reminders that, as Marcel Brion remarked, Joyce "creates his own time, as he creates his vocabulary and his characters. He soon elaborates what he receives from reality by a mysterious chemistry into new elements bearing the mark of this personality."[7] In a companion piece centered on the *Wake*'s conception of plot Elliot Paul noted, "If one can consider all events as having a standing regardless of date, that the happenings of all the years are taken from their place on the shelf and arranged, not in numerical order, but according to a design dictated by the mind of Joyce, then the text is not nearly so puzzling."[8]

The aforementioned use of nonmeaning or non-sense paradoxically employed to make a point leaps out at us on the final page of II.2. The described preparations for teatime are followed by an anticipatory countdown: "Aun / Do / Tri / Car" (308.05), and concluded by a "NIGHT-LETTER" containing Yuletide greetings to the parents from "jake, jack and little sousoucie / (the babes that mean too)" (308.23). But the ingratiating nature of the latter communication is shattered by the two concluding drawings at the bottom of the page. The first is a thumb to nose signifying the vulgar "kiss my ass," and the second represents crossed bones which seem to prophesy the coming of death. The figures are apparently drawn jointly by the children, since Issy "whopes he'll enjoyimsolff over our drawings on the line!" (308.fn). The effect of this upon the reader is much the same as the marbled page or the diagrams of plotline which Laurence Sterne offered in *Tristram Shandy*. The *Wake* drawings leap off the page to insult the reader, as well as a character or two, and we must suddenly redefine our relationship with the text. The joke is on us, as we pause in recognition of the fact that the page has recognized our existence and has made us a part of the proceedings. Since the chapter ends in a way which is totally unexpected, we must stop and recompose ourselves before moving on.

The step backward needed to comprehend the reversal in the

flow of Wakean narrative might be facilitated by another comment made by Elliot Paul: "If Noah, Premier Gladstone and 'Papa' Browning are telescoped into one, because of common characteristics, no violence is done to logic."[9] The *Wake* contains several overlying structural symbols or metaphors, such as the Letter, the Riddle, the Sin, and the Fall; another all-important one is the Telescope. Certainly the initial or primary function of a telescope is to see something which is far away more clearly. The Willingdone spies on the temptress Jinnies with a telescope of "Sex-caliber hrosspower" (8.36), and Shaun accuses Shem of the same sort of voyeurism: "he did take a tompip peepestrella throug a threedraw eighteen hawkspower durdicky telescope" (178.26). Buckley uses the instrument to catch sight of the Russian General, and the narrator's caution as to how we should read the Letter which the Hen found could easily be applied as well to the entirety of the plotline: "the farther back we manage to wiggle the more we need the loan of a lens to see as much as the hen saw" (112.01). The action of the *Wake,* such as it is, has been reversed and distanced, or at least separated from us by the shifting devices of narrative technique, so that we would probably agree with Shem's comment in the Lessons chapter: "When I'm dreaming back like that I begins to see we're only all telescopes" (295.10).

Things are transformed, of course, as much as they remain the same, and in the same chapter the twins' attempt at solving the mystery of their mother's vagina, as well as their geometry homework, is described as *"Two makes a wing at the macroscope telluspeep"* (275.L). Here the telescope becomes a microscope, as two functions of perception are fused into one—the twins are trying to see from near and from afar at the same time. The essential statement is that if we or they will only look in a new way, "peep," something important will be revealed, something will "tellus" what we want to know. The primary emphasis, then, is upon focusing, upon reversing direction, upon magnification, sometimes to the benefit of the scientist and sometimes to the benefit of the Peeping Tom.[10]

Examining the Telescope from another angle, its meaning as a verb can help to explain how and why Joyce is manipulating time and space shifts within the somewhat realistic portions of the narrative. To telescope something is to elongate it or to shorten it, as the instrument is expanded or contracted.(The sexual possibilities in this context are obvious.) If the main thing is to see something in its totality, which goahead plot apparently will not allow, any event must then be seen both from close up and from far away. The twins, for example, cannot appear only as boys of about fifteen years of age (483.21). To telescope them into a oneness of being, they must also function as very young children, as in III.4, or as mature adults, as in III.1. Even more comprehensively, they must be shown in varying phases of age in a single episode, as they are in II.1, the Mime of Mick, Nick, and the Maggies. Joyce accomplishes this by concentrating or elongating the segments of their ages as one would a telescope. In *Finnegans Wake,* age, like time, is fluid, can be telescoped, and characters reveal themselves to us from many points of view in any given moment.

In yet another letter sent to Harriet Shaw Weaver, Paul Leon feared that "The publication [of Work in Progress] in the opinion of many . . . will lead to a general and very strong onslaught on the part of the younger generation of left and communist linkings which will seize the opportunity to launch the rampant accusation that Mr. Joyce is in the service of capitalist art accessible only to the idle few and rich."[11] The younger generation does not seem to have been moved enough to become involved in this literary issue, but the problem of accessibility can never be separated from *Finnegans Wake.* Returning to the complications of plot, we must again admit that the narrative frustrates our expectations at every turn. The whole of Book I is a prime example, since it takes its own good time about letting a reader know just what the novel is supposed to be about. This Book takes the shape of a funnel, or a Dedalian tundish, in that we begin in the mists of protohistory, move through vague geneaologies, rumors and gossip, and must wait for chapters 6, 7, and 8 before anything like even a hazy picture of the cast of characters begins to emerge.

The first few chapters serve as a kind of crash course in Wakean technique which are meant to prepare us for even more convolution and manipulation which is to come. "To begin my life with the beginning of my life, I record that I was born (as I have been informed and believe) on a Friday, at twelve o'clock at night," states David Copperfield to begin his story. The protagonist of *Great Expectations* tries to be just as specific: "My father's family name being Pirrip, and my christian name Philip, my infant tongue could make of both names nothing longer or more explicit than Pip. So, I called myself Pip, and came to be called Pip." The first page of *Finnegans Wake* offers a character, Sir Tristram, who disappears after one paragraph, never to be seen in this guise again, and a spatial location of "this side the scraggy isthmus of Europe Minor" (3.05), combined with the temporal "not yet, though venissoon after, had a kidscad buttended a bland old isaac" (3.10). Even the dislocation of a moocow would be welcome here.

The narrative of the first chapter does not move logically from one place to another, but instead it is episodic and assembles what seem to be random bits and pieces. The introduction of Sir Tristram is followed by a description of a fall, by the funeral of Tim Finnegan, by a tour of the Willingdone Museyroom, by an Edenic interlude, by more protohistory, and by the confrontation of the Godotian Mutt and Jute. The narrator pauses to entreat our patience and attention—"Lissom! lissom! I am doing it" (21.02)—but immediately we are plunged into the fable of the Prankquean and just as quickly returned to the quasi-resurgent Finnegan being calmed at his own wake by a mourner. "Now be aisy, good Mr Finnimore, sir. . . . You're better off, sir, where you are" (24.16); "I've an eye on queer Behan and old Kate and the butter, trust me" (27.31). As will-of-the wisp characters like "Humme the Cheapner, Esc" (29.18) and "addle liddle phifie Annie" (4.28) float by, the acrostic implications of their names will certainly allude to HCE and ALP, but we can only discover this facet of the tale the second time around. Humphrey Chimpden remains unnamed and unmentioned specifically until I.2, and we have little solid narrational ground to stand on. Though we cannot know it yet, the chapter's final vignette of an ALP-like woman, "Airwinger's bride . . . reading her Evening World" (28.15), is an encapsulation of the entire chronicle of the book's events. The newspaper contains "News, news, all the news" (28.21), rumors about HCE, and a titillating serial about the lives and loves of Shem, Shaun, and Issy, and it closes with a mini-version of Anna Livia's final speech as river spirit: "There'll be bluebells blowing in salty sepulchres the night she signs her final tear. Zee end. But that's a world of ways away" (28.27). Jumbled plot and character will not respond to the critical eye in ways in which we have been led to expect.

It is interesting also to note some of the places where the narrative's direction is consistently deflected from the supposed subject at hand. I.2 begins with an explication of the events which, far back in history, led to the naming of Humphrey Chimpden Earwicker, and the section purports to be a brief in support of "the christlikeness of the big cleanminded giant H. C. Earwicker" (33.29). The cornerstone of the chapter is HCE's meeting with the Cad in Phoenix Park, described in the usual innocent–guilty terms. But, rather than concentrating on the confrontation between the two, the narrative focus is decoyed away from the protagonist into a wild-goose chase of rumors circulating around Dublin concerning the incident. HCE and his sin or lack of it get lost in the shuffle of gossip oscillating from the Cad's wife Lily Kinsella to a Browne-Nolan priest to Philly Thurston to Treacle Tom and Frisky Shorty. The tale is expanded by Peter Cloran and O'Mara, also known as Mildew Lisa, until the infamous Hosty composes the ballad which, through a French translation, transforms Earwicker's name into Persse O'Reilly. The problem in the Park is now revealed as "he was, in fact, in the habit of frequenting common lodginghouses where he slept in a nude state, hailfellow with meth, in strange men's cots" (39.30). The initial investigation (what is his name and what happened in the Park?) has slipped through our fingers, and the narrative offers answers which are preposterous. This refusal or inability to concentrate for long upon a difficulty which the narrative itself has proposed is endemic to the convoluted process of *Wake* telling.

In I.3, the rumors concerning HCE build to the ridiculous, while the inquisitive narrational voice attempts to hold the text to the business at hand with an assumption of formality: "But resuming inquiries" (66.10); "To proceed" (67.07); "Now to the obverse" (67.28); "Now by memory inspired" (69.05). The long list of abusive names he has been called at various times would seem to narrow the search, but, instead, we are led to conclude that at this stage even language itself will not do: "Words weigh no more to him than raindrips to Rethfernhim" (74.16). The narrator appears to reflect the reader's predicament, as he, she, or it falls gently asleep: "Rain. When we sleep. Drops. But wait until our sleeping. Drain. Sdops" (74.18). A growing irritability can be felt throughout the first half of Book I with conventional critical tools of explication. The narrative quite simply drowns us in details, superfluous or central we cannot ascertain, a relentless deluge of information which cries out for any sort of resolution: "Let us leave theories there and return to here's here" (76.10). The first four chapters of the novel are a testing ground of the viability of the method of investigation exemplified by the Aristotelian syllogism, and the Stagirite comes up short. Goahead plot has been fractured into runaway spirals which defy the organizing principle which our minds strive to impose.

Book I, then, breaks into two sections, the first four chapters a scattering of supposedly factual fragments which the final four will try to reassemble on a different level. A last chaotic case-in-point is I.4, which goes over once again the ground covered in I.2 with the confrontation in the Park. Now the action is intensified, as the HCE figure struggles with a robber armed with a gun who is looking for money with which to buy some Irish whisky. There is no mention of the time or any sort of sexual transgression, and, when it appears that the victim is penniless, the two part bloodied but amicable: "the queer mixture exchanged the pax in embrace or poghue puxy as practiced between brothers of the same breast" (83.32). On second thought, however, the victim complains to the police, and the arrest of one Festy King brings on a trial which promises to sort out matters.

Even though the reader is cautioned not to race ahead too quickly, that the direction of attention should not be forward but

"wurming along gradually for our savings backtowards mother-
waters so many miles from bank and Dublin stone" (84.30), the
hope remains that the problem will be settled. But the plot has
slipped a notch, now seems to center upon the brothers instead of
the father, and the characters themselves shift identities rapidly.
King is revealed to go about under several aliases (Crowbar,
Meleky, Tykingfest, and Rabworc) and denies everything. A surprise witness, who is identified as someone called the Wet Pinter,
says that there were three assailants rather than one, "the treepar-
tied ambush" (87.35). It may have been too dark to see clearly, but
he identifies the injured party as HERE COMES EVERYBODY
(88.21).

Again Joyce teases with allusion which never reveals its source,
and cross-examination of the Wet Pinter leads nowhere and everywhere: "And if it was all about that, egregious sir? About that and
the other" (90.20). The testimony races to an end with the explo-
sion of the archetypal thunderclap and an inconclusively conclusive
"You have it alright" (90.33). Statements become vaguer and
vaguer as King returns to the witness stand as Peggy Festy, and
meaning, along with plot direction, disintegrates into literal chaos.
Festy, revealed as "Show'm the Posed" (92.13), is feted by the
leapyear girls, while the Pinter, "Shun the Punman" (93.13), is
scorned. The four judges are at sixes and sevens, the Earwicker
figure has disappeared, and the conclusion of the section is as
meaningless as the preceding episode: "What was it? / A.........! /
?........O! / So there you are now" (94.20).

Obviously, I do not understand this story on a literal level, and I
do not believe that we are expected to. It is alpha and omega, the
beginning and the end, everything and nothing. A female figure
appears in a consoling guise, but narrative has come to a standstill,
a blind alley, and it virtually admits the fact. At this point conventional narrative has been stretched to its limit and snaps. *Finnegans Wake* will begin again through the remaining chapters of
Book I on a different level, as Joyce turns to the working out of
what he called in a letter to Miss Weaver "a picture-history from the
family album . . . and the ⋔ Δ household etc."[12]

If these concluding four chapters can be seen as a unit or a block of narration which seeks to discover a more viable way of getting through to the Earwickers,[13] it is significant that the narrator employs Anna Livia as a framing device. Her letter will be discussed in I.5 and her history in I.8. It is almost as if the narrative voice reflects the realization that things have broken down and will start over with an examination of the basic influence of the female principle. The narrational tone is much more conciliatory to the reader, and the catalogue of the many titles which the manafesta has received is followed by counsel: "Now, patience; and remember patience is the great thing, and above all things else we must avoid anything like being or becoming out of patience" (108.08). This is not to say that I.5 is somehow easier to penetrate than what has gone before, but at least the narrative focus remains pretty much centered upon the Letter for the bulk of the chapter. The Letter can provide entrance into the family and is decipherable. This pseudo-examination of a pseudo-text is somehow reassuringly familiar.

One salient aspect of the *Wake* is that it is usually a series of incidents or mini-plots strung together and related to moments in the Earwicker's lives, much like the structure of the Circe chapter in *Ulysses*. Consequently, the reader's attention is constantly distracted, having to adjust to the jump from one little story and cast of characters to another. Here in I.5, at least, the extended discussion provides a consistent and lengthy ground for critical exploration, and it even begins to move closer to the primary characters.

The narrator provides us with an introduction to the Earwickers and their individual symbols, beginning with "the initials majuscle of Earwicker: the meant to be baffling chrismon trilithon sign ᛘ" (119.16), and continues with the identifying marks of the rest of the family. (These, of course, are the symbols which Joyce himself used in his notebooks and correspondence.) The reader is treated with sympathy: "You is feeling like you was lost in the bush, boy?. . . . You most shouts out: Bethicket me for a stump of a beech if I have the poultriest notions what the farest he all means" (112.03). We are strongly encouraged not to give up hope: "so holp me Petault, it is not a miseffectual whyacinthinous riot of blots and blurs and bars and balls and hoops and wriggles and juxtaposed jottings linked by spurts of speed: it only looks as like it as damn it" (118.28).

In many ways, I.5 is a lesson in reading which is meant to set us up for the rest of the novel: "one who deeper thinks will always bear in the baccbuccus of his mind that this downright there you are and there it is is only all in his eye" (118.15). What is needed for this "ideal reader suffering from an ideal insomnia" (120.13) is the ability to "here keen again and begin again to make soundsense and sensesound kin again" (121.14). With cautions such as these in mind, we are supposed to be ready to proceed directly to the puzzles of I.6.

The so-called Questions chapter, which Clive Hart says "represents the Dreamer's most honest and directly introverted consideration of his present dreaming state,"[14] demonstrates a major change in the method and direction of the narrative. Finally we are to be given descriptions of the characters, including views of several of the supporting players, and we can hear echoes of their individual voices, if not necessarily transcriptions of the real thing. The narrator has slipped behind the stage curtain, allowing Shem to pose twelve questions, eight of which are answered by Shaun and one each by Mamalujo, Kate the Slops, Issy, and Shem himself. This longest section of the Book is the children's chapter which sneaks a look at the parents, introduces the household, and solidifies the brother rivalry. These pictures from the family album defy any forward motion of the narrative just as much as the previous chapters did, but they serve to provide specific pegs upon which the reader can hang the strings of archetypal allusions and situations which have been collecting since the first page of *Finnegan Wake*.

The two fables which Shaun tells about the Mookse and the Gripes and Burrus and Caseous are now locatable in their relationship to the Earwicker twins, as perhaps Mutt and Jute initially were not, and Nuvoletta and Margareena are identifiable as Issy. The ninth question, which goes on to ask just what is this unfolding text all about—"*what* would that fargazer seem to seemself to seem seeming of, dimm it all?" (143.26)—is answered by "A collideorscape!" (143.28). The emphasis on "seem" may be tentative, but the image of the kaleidoscope, with further connotations of the Telescope and of shifting patterns and colliding meteors, is a solid hint at the construction and the structure of the narration. The perspective of the fictional funnel has finally trickled down to the family we have come to investigate, and chapters 7 and 8 will fill in a little more background.

The caricature of Shem with all his warts—and limned in by Shaun—is curious, not only because of the vitriol of Shaun's diatribe, but also because we are confronted by a full-grown man rather than the boy we had been led to expect. Joyce brings into play the sliding scale of age once again. The *Wake* opens up another dimension of the significance of this "mental and moral defective" (177.16) when it becomes clear that Shem is also a portrait of the artist himself. Shem enjoys reading his own *Ulysses,* "telling himself delightedly, no espellor mor so, that every splurge on the vellum he blundered over was an aisling vision more gorgeous than the one before" (179.29). Even Laurence Sterne was not quite capable of something like this.[15]

Behind Shem stands Shaun, behind him the nameless narrator, and behind them all a self-mocking James Joyce peeps out. Characterization has become so fluid that its application can now be almost universal. (Another game the reader can play is to search for his or her own name in the text, and almost always some form of it will be there.)

The JUSTIUS-MERCIUS counterstatements at the end of the chapter seek firmly to establish the moral positions of the twins, if nothing else, but even here nothing is conventionally stable. Shaun remains Shaun—"Sh! Shem, you are. Sh! You are mad!" (193.27)—but Shem as MERCIUS begins to blend into his mother: "because ye left from me, because ye laughed on me, because, O me lonly son, ye are forgetting me!, that our turfbrown mummy is acoming" (194.20). "Here I am. Look at me," sings a chorus composed of characters and author.

Once again, there is no elaboration of plot as such, as there will be none in the Anna Livia chapter. There are stories, but no history or biography which has a realistic–fictional base. The catalogue of the names of the games the boys liked to play (176) is matched by the list of ALP's presents and their recipients (210–211). The washer-woman's call to her partner to tell all about Anna Livia results initially in talk of the husband. The demand for more plot telling, "Where did I stop? Never stop! Continuarration! You're not there yet. I amstel waiting" (205.13), is answered by singsong nursery rhymes to fill up the space: "This is the Hausman all paven and stoned, that cribbed the Cabin that never was owned that cocked his leg and hennad his Egg" (205.34).

The style of these two chapters is gossipaceous, almost run-on, but the narrative thrust is actually once again backwards. The song sung after a soccer match, during which Shem was supposedly beaten up, is described by Joseph Campbell and Henry Morton Robinson as "a combination and modification of the *recorso* paragraph of page 3 and the ballad of 'Persse O'Reilly.' "[16] This is undoubtedly true, but the center of the poem or song also contains lines which recapitulate most of the events of the entire first chapter:

> *Not yet has the emp from Corpsica forced the Arth out of Engleterre;*
> *Not yet have the Sachsen and Judder on the Mound of a Word made Warre;*
> *Not yet Witchywitchy of Wench struck Fire of his Heath from on Hoath;*
> *Not yet his Arcobaleine forespoken Peacepeace upon Oath;* (175.11).

The first quoted line is the Museyroom, the second the Mutt and Jute dialogue, the third and fourth recall the Prankquean and Jarl von Hoother, and the rest of the song is a restatement of the wake festivities. Back we go, once again.

In the same fashion, the washer-women's discussion of Anna Livia's first lover is backward from "a dynast of Leinster, a wolf of the sea" (202.24), to "a heavy trudging lurching lieabroad of a Curraghman. . . . You're wrong there, corribly wrong! Tisn't only tonight you're anacheronistic! It was ages behind that" (202.29). We continue back in time through several more possibilities to the hermit priest Michael Arklow, to two boys named Barefoot Burn and Wallowme Wade. Before that "she was licked by a hound, Chirripa-Chirruta, while posing her pee, pure and simple" (204.11), though finally it appears that she was seduced by the Liffey River itself in some sort of Zeuslike metamorphosis. "The cords of all link back," (*Ulysses,* 32.37) thought Stephen Dedalus.

Much as a mirror throws back an image which moves as the reflected figures move, these family pictures will not remain static, almost as if each can be peeled off the album page to reveal another behind it. Book I moves from generalization to specificity in its plot focusing, but this is a specificity which demands constant reorganization in the reader's mind. In many ways, Book I is yet another end and a beginning. It is an introduction to many of the plot devices which Joyce will manipulate to produce a new kind of technique of reading, but it is also something of a tease since only a few of the author's narrational surprises have been pulled out of the bag. We seem to have a cast of characters now, but all we really see arc colorful shapes which will not coalesce into a central figure. Point of view will not remain fixed, plot will not unfold, and speakers are to be mistrusted. Both writer and reader might be aptly described as "any usual sort of ornery josser, flatchested fortyish, faintly flatulent and given to ratiocination by syncopation in the elucidation of complications" (109.03). Goahead plot has long ago been discarded and forgotten, and the reader must turn back to the family album to forge ahead.

3

There Are Sordidly Tales within Tales
(522.05)

With the opening of Book II, the plot begins to goahead at a quicker rate, but Joyce will bring to bear several structural devices which we have not seen before to hold things firmly together. While the members of the Earwicker family, and especially the children, will step into the foreground, the narrator emerges as the force which attempts to maintain complete control of the shaping of the narrative material. It is almost as if the characters have begun to develop wills of their own, so that the narrator must strive constantly to hold them in check, to direct their appearances and exits, and to move them firmly toward appropriate conclusions. Consequently, the rest of *Finnegans Wake* will display a cornucopia of narrational forms, a different approach in virtually each succeeding chapter, before Anna Livia as the Liffey River will ultimately merge with the sea.

Though Shaun and the washerwomen were allowed to speak fairly freely in Book I, so that they moved the plot along in what seemed to be any direction they wished, this will be the case no longer. The narrator does his best in his new role as a formal taskmaster. In its multiplicity of styles and strategies, *Finnegans Wake* mirrors *Ulysses* in its insistence on the artificiality of its own high art.

By now it is generally accepted that we need pay little attention to the assertion of Stephen Dedalus in *A Portrait of the Artist* that all art is either lyrical, epic, or dramatic. With such a paradigm, Joyce's works fit this pattern, thus making *Finnegans Wake* dramatic. Though the entire idea is too neat, it is true that Joyce will utilize a dramatic form quite frequently in organizing his narrational material. Although the Prankquean's fable, for example, was introduced with a stock situational tag—"It was of a night, late, lang time agone, in a aulstane eld, when Adam was delvin and his madameen spinning watersilts" (21.051)—the Mime of Mick, Nick, and the Maggies (II.2) is produced in full dramatic regalia. Once again we begin with a setting in time and space, "Every evening at lighting up o'clock sharp and until further notice in Feenichts Playhouse" (219.01), but our narrator continues with a complete set of stage directions and an extended account of the dramatis personae. In something of a curious way, the cast of characters will include all of those about to perform (Shem is Glugg, Shaun is Chuff, and Issy is Izod or Miss Butys Pott), but it also mentions Kate, the Man of All Work, and the customers in HCE's pub, none of whom will participate.

There still remains a screen between the Earwickers and fictional reality. Perhaps the narrator wishes to make sure that at least he knows the whereabouts of everyone concerned. Joyce informed Harriet Shaw Weaver that this chapter was an account of the children at play, and he provided an outline of each of the four chapters which would make up the whole of Book II. There is a plot to be unraveled here, or at least a series of events to be viewed, but everything is complicated by the realization that several layers of audience stand between the theatergoer and the play.

Nathan Halper has this to say: "To understand the book, no matter how imperfectly, we must see it as a whole. To see it as a whole—no matter how imperfectly—we must acquire a sense of the little world of Earwicker. Here and there in the book, Joyce has hidden the material with which we may build it."[1] To distance the reader from the action, Joyce employed complications of style in *Ulysses,* and in the *Wake* we must look over the shoulders of several characters who sit in front of us and of a narrator who conspicuously maneuvers the scenery. Thus Joyce's director informs us of his stage technique every step of the way. We learn that movies and their cameras have an influence on the staging: "Shadows by the film folk, masses by the good people . . . upcloses, outblacks and stagetolets by Hexenschuss, Coachmaher, Incubone and Rocknarrag" (221.21). We are carefully introduced to the narrative: "An argument follows" (222.21); "Towhere byhangs ourtales" (224.08); "A pause" (235.06). Asides often function as cues for the reader: "There lies her word, you reder!" (249.13); "in the ersebest idiom I have done it equals I so shall do [past equals future] . . . look at me now means I once was otherwise [present equals past]" (253.01).

Any conventional movement toward suspension of disbelief is upset by an intentional clumsiness or perhaps sincerity in describing how the props and characters get from one place to another: "the producer (Mr. John Baptister Vickar) caused a deep abuliousness to descend upon the Father of Truants" (255.27). In fact, of course, this is not precisely drama or dramatic at all but is instead prose narrative with a collection of theatrical trappings which enshroud it. The antics of the children and the presentation of the rivalry of Shem and Shaun are carried out behind the facade of the riddling game. With a decided thumbing of the nose, this time directed at the Bard of Avon—"You're well held now, Missy Cheekspeer, and your panto's off" (257.20)—the play collapses into another thunderclap. Nothing remains for the narrator to do but to turn out the lights: "Upploud! The play thou schouwburgst, Game, here endeth. The curtain drops by deep request" (257.30).[2]

It should be noted as well, though, that drama in the *Wake* is not simply or only farce. The struggle of Shem and Shaun in the Mime was passed off by Joyce thusly: "The scheme of the piece I sent you is the game we used to call Angels and Devils or colours,"[3] but this section deals with a crucial aspect of the narrative—brother striving against brother to win the affections of the female. In parallel instances of the sibling confrontation, like Kersse the Tailor and the Norwegian Captain and the Ondt and the Gracehoper, Joyce will manipulate a dramatic structure, perhaps to underscore the seriousness of his subject. In an early essay, "Drama and Life," he said, "Drama has to do with the underlying laws first, in all their nakedness and divine severity, and only secondarily with the motley agents who bear them out."[4] He went on to assert that "here the artist forgoes his very self and stands a mediator in awful truth before the veiled face of God."

We know that Joyce agreed with the philosophy expressed by Nietzsche in *The Birth of Tragedy* on the quintessential ritualistic, mythic nature of the drama, and perhaps something of this ingrained respect remains in virtually every one of *Finnegans Wake*'s theater pieces. While keeping in mind the comic accoutrements of the cavalcade of "motley agents," we must acknowledge along with them the somewhat serious codas of each drama. Vincent Cheng states, "In a chronicle of history, all the activities of life are sooner or later portrayed in dramatic terms,"[5] and perhaps it is not too much to say that Joyce's endings embody this concept.

The Mime concludes with a prayer of benediction, and the gravity of its tone, replete with Biblical intonations, is in sharp contrast to the mocking voice which described the events which have come before.[6] Though the Lord has become the "Loud," one can perceive that the closure is meant to be treated with sympathy. "Thou hast closed the portals of the habitations of thy children and thou hast set the guards thereby, even Garda Didymus and Garda Domas, that thy children may read in the book of the opening of the mind to light and err not in the darkness which is the afterthought of thy nomatter by the guardiance of those guards which are thy bodemen" (258.28).

It does seem that whenever the conventional elements of plot, the actual doings of the Earwickers, almost manage to poke their heads above the surface of the Wakean night, the narrator will not dismiss them so flippantly or easily. This is certainly not intended as the beginning of a brief on Joyce's solemnity or his belief in a higher being (perish the thought), but he does not always look at his characters with a cynical laugh. The artificiality of the staging of the Mime is balanced by a blessing which is only a step or two away from sentimentality: "O Loud, hear the wee beseech of thees of each of these thy unlitten ones!" (259.03). Joyce here mediates between the Loud and the little ones, and the drama describes their essential inseparability. We might note that the same paradoxical tone of somewhat playful religiosity concludes the dramatic fable of the Ondt and the Gracehoper: "In the name of the former and of the latter and of their holocaust. Allmen" (419.09).

The dramatic form is complicated even more in III.4, where HCE and Anna Livia are awakened from their slumbers by Shem's nightmare, and they return to bed to make love in what might be called "the Strangest Dream that was ever Halfdreamt" (307.11). The long opening sentence (555–558) which introduces the family, again as dramatic personae, ends in confusion: "Where are we at all? and whenabouts in the name of space? I don't understand. I fail to say. I dearsee you too" (558.33). The conventional locating of the narrative in time and space has not succeeded, and the narrator imposes a dramatic structure to bring about order and to reassure the reader. But, along with the formal stage directions—"Scene and property plot. Stagemanager's prompt. Interior of dwelling on outskirts of city" (558.35)—the narrator experiments even further by bringing into play the perspectives and comments of the Four, Mamalujo, usually regarded in this context as the four bedposts.

What results is a tension, or even comic contrast, created by the spareness of the narrator's directorial tone and the folksy ramblings of the garrulous old historians. Thus, "Man with nightcap, in bed, fore. Woman, with curlpins, hind. Discovered. Side point of view. First position of harmony" (559.20), is counterpointed by a description like this of Anna Livia's hurrying to the room of Shem: "By the sinewy forequarters of the mare Pocahontas and by the white shoulders of Finnuala you should have seen how that smart sallow lass just hopped a nanny's gambit out of bunk like old mother Mesopotomac" (559.32). No matter how much the narrator attempts to hurry things along with exposition, the gossipy old men will pause to smell the flowers and inadvertently foil or postpone the goahead plot.

Again the narrator squares things away for progression—"Shifting scene. Wall flats: sink and fly. Spotlight working wall cloths" (560.04)—and again Matt the narrational tourist, charmed by what he sees around him, provides what approaches an advertisement for the real estate: "What scenic artist! It is ideal residence for realtar" (560.13). Like the irritating theatergoer in the seat in front of us who would rather chat with his neighbor than watch the play, Matt begins a friendly conversation. "Tell me something. The Porters, so to speak, after their shadowstealers in the newsbaggers, are very nice people, are they not?" (560.22). In a very strange way, as he suddenly turns his attention to the narrator, Mark distracts our formalist guide away from the matter at hand and leads him into a dialogue which is centered upon the dramatic action.

As the Earwicker characters go about their business, they are commented upon by our audience of two, while the reader eavesdrops and overhears. The scene of the sleeping children so enthralls the narrator that he has to be warned not to get too close to Issy—"Approach not for ghost sake! It is dormition!" (561.27)—and not to make any sudden noise in front of Shaun: "Do you not waken him! Our farheard bode. He is happily to sleep" (562.23).

Beginning as the director, the narrator quickly assumes the role of a passive spectator. Matt's parting blessing, "Adieu, soft adieu, for these nice presents, kerryjevin. Still tosorrow!" (563.35), sends the narrator scurrying along to the second old man for more information. "What is the view which now takes up a second position of discordance, tell it please? Mark! You notice it in that rereway because the male entail partially eclipses the femecovert" (564.01).

Mark, after satisfying more of the narrator's questions, and even offering him a Guinness for his nerves, gets to oversee a major moment in the drama: Anna Livia's comforting of Shem. We, as the audience twice removed, are afforded two of the mother's speeches as she calms the child, but these are punctuated by Mamlujo's asking each in Esperanto what all the trouble is about. None of the guides seems to be able to concentrate for long on what is happening on the stage, and, just as Matt praised the real estate, Mark launches into a puff for the pub. "When you're coaching through Lucalised, on the sulphur spa to visit, it's safer to hit than miss it, stop at his inn!" (565.33).

So the reader must concentrate on two simultaneous series of events or dialogues while the primary level of event that we so desperately wish to view—what is going on with the Earwickers—is clouded and distorted by the whims of the secondary characters who frustrate our desire to know.

An additional problem is that Mark, in good-old-prim-yet-prying Mamlujo style, attempts to censor any prurient occurrence while he peeps at it at the same time. When Earwicker inadvertantly reveals his erection, the narrator objects to such a graphic display: "What do you show on?" (566.33). Mark replies apologetically that he is obliged to recount what he sees: "I show because I must see before my misfortune so a stark pointing pole. Lord of ladders, what for lungitube!" (566.33) A bit carried away, Mark comments further on size and length, until the narrator complains once more, "At that do you leer, a setting up? With a such unfettered belly?" (567.05). At this point, Mark can only confess his unabashed interest: "I leer (O my big, O my bog, O my bigbagbone!) because I must see a buntingcap of so a pinky on the point" (567.06). Any sort of control of the narration which the narrator may have possessed at the beginning of this household drama has long since disappeared.

Recovering himself, Mark continues with paeans to HCE and ALP which culminate in bell-ringing celebrations in fifteen Dublin churches, and he contemplates constructing yet another play to honor the happy couple. "Mumm me moe mummers! . . . Play actors by us ever have crash to their gate" (569.28). (As we probably might expect, along with several other variant titles for the proposed piece, Mark includes: "two genitalmen of Veruno" [569.31]). The dialogue between the historian and the narrator begins once again, in an attempt to continue on something of a more serious level, as the narrator is asked about HCE's physical condition: "Vouchsafe me more soundpicture! It gives furiously to think. Is rich Mr Pornter, a squire, not always in his such strong health?" (570.14).

Our two guides and their perambulations have replaced the Earwickers as the center of attention. Try as he might to control himself, Mark must break down into laughter once more at the sight of the naked mother and father. "She, she, she! But on what do you again leer? I am not leering, I pink you pardons. I am highly sheshe sherious" (570.24). The narrator asks if Mark is in need of a bathroom before he wets his pants, and the latter agrees that this is a possibility, but the latter-day evangelist manages to get hold of himself. The process of narration takes precedence over the individual acts of the narrative themselves, and dramatic form has become essentially conversational. No one entity is in control, and, after two snatches of muttered dialogue between the parents, confusion reigns.

The narrative level flips back to I.8, the Anna Livia section, for a moment, and the chaos is complete: "Cant ear! Her dorters ofe? Whofe? Her eskmeno daughters hope? Whope? Ellme, elmme, elskmestoon! Soon! (572.16). As we have seen before and will see again, such an echo of a previous chapter of the *Wake* enjoins the reader to turn back in order to understand what is to come. One conversation about the Earwickers is all conversations about the Earwickers, something to be remembered before the resumption of goahead plot.

Fritz Senn cautions rightly and wisely about critical discussions of this type. "I would simply argue for more care in the articulation of our observations. A little more reticence, perhaps, when we use formulas like '*Finnegans Wake* is . . .,' for it is not, even if it may be useful to treat it as though it were, for the moment. As long as we know what we are doing the damage is minimal."[7] For the moment, then, I would say that *Finnegans Wake is* a novel of talk. Thus we have discussions between the Mookse and the Gripes, the two washerwomen, Butt and Taff, the Ondt and the Gracehoper, and the Archdruid Berkeley and Saint Patrick, to name only a few.

Whatever the subject at hand, it is advanced primarily through conversation between the characters. In the Museyroom we have one guide, Kate, and one exhibit to contemplate. Here, in III.4 (in the Earwicker's bedroom) we have two chattering commentators and a living, dramatic tableau, but the dramatic tension is generated by the interplay of the two guides, one comic and one serious, describing the play in ways which each considers proper. Given the conflict between these narrative voices, often vivid and highly emotional, it is quite easy to forget momentarily about the action transpiring at the back of the stage. An extended explication of this kind is often necessary to keep track of the several narrational balls which Joyce the juggler is manipulating in the Wakean air.

When we discuss *Finnegans Wake,* it is always better to describe it with an analogy rather than a definition, and an apt one is supplied by Sylvia Beach. She recalls talking to Joyce when he was in the middle of writing his novel, and he mentioned that "history was like that parlor game where someone whispers something to the person next to him, who repeats it not very distinctly to the next person, and so on until, by the time the last person hears it, it comes out completely transformed."[8] In many ways, this is exactly what happens with Wakean narrative and the Earwickers' own fictional history.

Thus, the aforementioned reversion to the language of the washerwomen causes the narrator to take back responsibility from the evangelist and to present the highly respectable legal document of the marital dispute of Honuphrius and Anita. "Has he hegemony and shall she submit?" (573.32). In typical fashion, the narrative is suspended by an extended aside which takes us above and beyond the Earwickers, while Mark is momentarily silenced. This pause in the plot seems to set the narrative back on course, and bits and pieces of the parents' discussing their return to bed conclude with Anna Livia's benediction for the sleeping Shem. "While hovering dreamwings, folding around, will hide from fears my wee mee mannikin, keep my big wig long strong manomen, guard my bairn" (576.14). The poignancy and sincerity of this domestic statement inspire in the narrator the same sort of momentary reverence we saw in the Mime, and he calls upon a God of sorts. "Prospector projector and boomooster giant builder of all causeways woesoever" (576.18) to bless them.

The hilarity and even farce of the previous scenes are replaced by a prayer whose seriousness is perhaps meant to reassert the underlying significance of the connubial drama, and this prayer continues for almost two entire pages. Its tenor sounds convincing (for the most part): "Prick this man and tittup this woman, our forced payrents. . . . Bit Maester Finnykin with Phenicia Parkes . . . we beseach of you, down their laddercase of nightwatch service and bring them at suntime flush with the nethermost gangrung of their stepchildren, guide them through the labyrinth of their samilikes and the alteregoases of their pseudoselves" (576.26).

Again, we should not push the gravity of the benediction too far, beyond noting that the narrator seems to have been taken up by the scene. He wishes of the pair "that he may dishcover her, that she may uncouple him, that one may come and crumple them, that they may soon recoup themselves" (577.18). In the imagery of the play, HCE and ALP are "Regies Producer with screendoll Vedette" (577.15), though in the cyclic nature of all existence in *Finnegans Wake* everything can finally be reduced or expanded to "curious dreamers, curious dramas" (577.32).

Certainly, Joyce will not allow this seriousness of tone to continue for any extended time, and Mark, quiescent for too long, entices the narrator back into conversation. In the *Wake,* the audience subverts the play, since even the producers and directors aspire to be players. Armed with a detailed and exhausting series of questions, like a child on a long and boring journey, Mark badgers for minutiae, so that the narrator must go so far as to describe what Earwicker has on his feet. "His feet wear doubled width socks for he always must to insure warm sleep between a pair of fully fleeced bankers like a finnoc in a cauwl" (578.08). Mark can only be silenced finally by a series of admonitory and even downright silly precepts. "Scrape your souls. Commit no miracles. Postpone no bills. Respect the uniform" (579.13).

We are finally moving toward the dramatic highpoint of this chapter, the sexual encounter of Humphrey Chimpden and Anna Livia, but the narrator is in no great hurry. He seems content, perhaps for reasons of delicacy, to put off the intimate moment, and he stops once again to eulogize them in language which at first elevates the couple as a pair of timeless, archetypal parents, and then almost makes them sound like characters in a Samuel Beckett novel. "For they met and mated and bedded and buckled and got and gave and reared and raised and brought Thawland within Har danger . . . and left off leaving off and kept on keeping on" (579.27). Ultimately, however, he will be forced, like it or not, to fulfill his role as the stagemanager and chronicler of events. "Ah ho! Say no more about it! I'm sorry! I saw. I'm sorry! I'm sorry to say I saw!" (581.24).

The narrator will do his best stylistically to back away from the copulation he must soon describe, and he attempts to dismiss the subject altogether. The scene is just not worth going into: "some togethergush of stillandbutallyouknow that" (581.27). The narrative voice, in its uneasiness and embarrassment, becomes more and more disjointed until, at the moment of truth, it simply cannot go on. The dramatic focus has shifted away from the play to the consternation in the mind and feelings of the narrator. In panic, our guide launches into a brand new story whose plot disintegrates into meaninglessness, as he flounders madly for something to say. "So there was a raughty . . . who in Dyfflinsborg did . . . [. . .] Where there was a fair young . . . Who was playing her game of . . . And she said you rockaby . . . Will you peddle in my bog [. . .] And that's how Humpfrey, champion emir, holds his own. Shysweet, she rests" (582.21). Obviously, however, these polite fragments from a book of master plots or how to tell a story just will not do, and neither we nor the narrator's associates are satisfied.

Though Mark may have retired from the fray, his compatriot Luke has not, and the latter steps to the fore and impatiently demands some action. "Or show pon him now, will you!" (582.28). From his perspective—"Third position of concord! Excellent view from front. Sidome. Female imperfectly masking male" (582.29)—Luke can see everything. He takes over the narration and exhorts the audience to "Gaze at him [HCE] now in momentum! . . . by the lee of his hulk upright on her orbits, and the heave of his juniper arx in action, he's naval I see" (582.36). The narrator retires for the nonce, and a general comment made by John Paul Riquelme may help to clarify some of the confusing narrational interchange: "The narrator's presence is of a structural sort, and that is an odd kind of presence indeed. It reveals itself through difference: through the difference between the character's interior voice and the surrounding narration and through the differences between styles as the narration proceeds from episode to episode."[9]

Luke's section contains a multiplicity of styles and imagery. The nautical language which he uses initially to describe the couple is soon transformed into the vernacular of horse racing. "The field is down, the race is their own. The galleonman jovial on his bucky brown nightmare. . . . And the twillingsons, ganymede, garrymore, turn in trot and trot. But old pairamere goes it a gallop, a gallop" (583.07). To color the event even more, Luke weaves into his description an abundance of references to cricket, and the lovemaking turns into a sporting event. In many ways III.4 is a mirror of II.4, and just as Mamalujo used soccer and horse racing to disguise the lovemaking of Tristan and Isolde there, so they resort to cricket and thoroughbred racing here. The scene was presented as drama there, and so too it is drama here.

Perhaps the key word in this context is the invidious "hesitancy." Though the Four openly leer as seagulls at Tristan and Isolde, they are not so completely salacious as they were previously. Luke may become momentarily quite graphic in his description of Anna Livia—"Tipatonguing him on in her pigeony linguish, with a flick at the bails for lubrication, to scorch her faster, faster" (584.03)— but the rest of the scene is cloaked in a language which, in its vagueness and almost non-sense, protects the parents from the gaze of the audience. "Echolo choree choroh choree chorico! How me O my youhou my I youtou to I O?" (585.03).

The bluntness of Tristan's conclusion borders on the crude: "they could hear like of a lisp lapsing, that was her knight of the truths thong plipping out of her chapellledeosy, after where he had gone and polped the questioned. Plop" (396.30). Now, though, Luke resorts to parliamentary language, and even manages to be funny. "O yes! O yes! Withdraw your member! Closure. This chamber stands abjourned" (585.26). Luke seems happy to get things over with and to draw back to a more philosophical, distanced position. The production is coming to a close, and it seems time to tie up loose ends and conclude. The silliness which we might usually associate with Mamalujo has at least momentarily been transcended. "This is seriously meant. . . . All in fact is soon as all of old right as anywas ever in very old place" (586.18).

Each of the three dramatic historians has proved to be a bit more sober about the narration than his predecessor, and Johnny is consistent with this pattern. It remains for him to conclude that "our Theoatre Regal's drolleries puntomine" (587.08), and he does so by eschewing any further recountings of action and by speaking or philosophizing directly to us, the audience. The coming together of Earwicker and Anna Livia is just more of the same old archetypal structure: "Since Allan Rogue loved Arrah Pogue it's all killdoughall fair" (588.28). We are asked to look back on the drama, to forget about goahead plot, to return to Earwicker as we would return to the beginning of a rainbow from back to front. HCE is "a chameleon at last, in his true falseheaven colours from ultraviolent to subred tissues" (590.07). It is left to Johnny to offer the audience, "Fourth position of solution. How johnny! Finest view from horizon. Tableau final" (590.22).

We have moved from harmony, to discordance, to concord, to solution, an apt definition of dramatic progression. With the coming of the dawn, the stage manager brings down the curtain, "Ring down" (590.27), and calls for applause like any good Elizabethan epiloguist. As the lights fade and the play ends, Earwicker can sleep: "While the queenbee he staggerhorned blesses her bliss for to feel her funnyman's functions" (590.27). The conclusion of this drama seems a satisfactory one for all concerned, and perhaps we too can rest in momentary resolution.

If the reader can pause for a second, however, he or she can only rest in retrospection. The concluding chapter of Book III recalls, as was mentioned before, the Tristan and Isolde coda of Book II and the washerwomen's discussion of Anna Livia and her husband which finishes Book I. Vladimir Nabokov noted that "Sequence arises only because words have to be written one after the other on consecutive pages, just as the reader's mind must have time to go through the book, at least the first time he reads it. . . . If the mind were constructed on optional lines and if a book could be read in the same way as a painting is taken in by the eye, that is without the bother of working from left to right and without the absurdity of beginnings and ends, this would be the ideal way of appreciating a novel, for thus the author saw it at the moment of its conception."[10]

The last line of III.4, "Tiers, tiers and tiers. Rounds" (590.30), would seem a cue to emphasize the synchronicity of what we have seen and points out the simultaneous nature of fictional events. "Tiers" is obviously a series of rows or ranks of seats in a theater, and also "tears" of sadness and "tierce," in card games a sequence of three cards in the same suit. If we can only turn round, we could apprehend the three sexual ages of the woman Anna Livia, from the young girl seduced by the Liffrey, to the "strapping modernold ancient Irish prisscess . . . [with] a firstclass pair of bedroom eyes, of most unhomy blue" (396.07), to the mature woman. If sex is dramatic, and apparently to Joyce it is, Anna Livia is to be perceived in the verticality of the little plays which document the progression of her fictional career. The "solution" of Johnny's final view is accomplished by looking back to the Anna Livias we have known before, while we prepare for the ultimate apotheosis which is to come in Book IV.

Despite the presence of Saint Kevin in his bathtub and the debate between Saint Patrick and the Archdruid Berkeley, the keystone of the final section remains Anna Livia. Her letter and her river speech are introduced by a statement which reminds us once again to turn back to understand the here and now: "Yet is no body present here which was not there before. Only is order othered" (613.13). Yet again, the narrator alludes to the washerwomen chapter in Book I: "Themes have thimes and habit reburns. To flame in you. Ardor vigor forders order. Since ancient was our living is in possible to be" (614.08).

The book almost seems to struggle against its own ending, and the narrator holds back from Anna Livia until he is sure that the audience is prepared. He anticipates our questions and provides us with answers before we ask. "What has gone? How it ends? Begin to forget it. It will remember itself from every sides, with all gestures, in each our word. Today's truth, tomorrow's trend. Forget, remember!" (614.19).

Anna Livia's letter (615.12–619.19) is in fact not a letter at all, despite its form, and is instead a dramatic monologue. Her speech is basically a combination of past and future tenses which encapsulates the paradoxical fusion of looking forward and back, which has been a central concern all along. "Yon clouds will soon disappear looking forwards at a fine day . . . as merrily we rolled along" (615.17). In its giddy gossip, the speech contains all that has gone before and all that will come again, when we read *Finnegans Wake* yet another time, and thus in its form it demonstrates the transcendence of goahead plot. We are warned not to make mistakes in identifying the characters—"they've changed their characticuls during their blackout" (617.13)—and are reminded of the essential admonition, "Don't forget! . . . Remember" (617.25).

The river-spirit speech which follows (619.20–628.16) manipulates the opposition of past, present, and future, since it is not, as we may have thought, simply Anna Livia's rejection of her husband and family. Also, it is not entirely correct to label the speaker the spirit of the Liffey, since this monologue on one level is rooted in the here and now of ALP in bed with HCE. This ultimate Wakean section begins with an Anna Livia awake and collecting her thoughts: "The childher are still fast. There is no school today. Them boys is so contrairy" (620.11). Then it returns to the past for recollections of her relationship with her husband: "But that night after, all you were wanton! Bidding me do this and that and the other. And blowing off to me, hugly Judsys, what wouldn't you give to have a girl! Your wish was mewill" (620.24).

At first it seems that the couple will proceed together on the archetypal journey, and preparations reflect a pragmatic and mundane concern with necessities. Anna Livia will need an addition to her wardrobe: "Only but, theres a but, you must buy me a fine new girdle too, nolly. When next you go to Market Norwall. They're all saying I need it since the one from Isaacsen's slooped its line" (621.17). Soon, however, it becomes clear that the female, metamorphosing at last into the stream, must go on ahead alone. There is something of a sentimental tone to the final pages: "You will always call me leafiest, won't you, dowling?" (624.22). The same watchword that was left for the reader, however, is what Anna Livia underlines for HCE. She calls upon him to turn back: "You remember?" (622.17), "Remember" (623.09), "Remember" (623.16).

Despite the imminence of a parting, of a voyage out, it is what has gone before which is of the utmost importance. "It is all so often and still the same to me. . . . You've never forgodden batt on tarf, have you" (625.16). Again and again she implores him, and the reader as well: "If I lose my breath for a minute or two don't speak, remember!" (625.28). We must return again like Dick Whittington "So side by side, turn agate weddingtown, laud men of Londub!" (625.35). Read from left to right, a combination of London and Dublin, "Londub" becomes simply Dublin itself from a reverse direction. Here, as Joyce demonstrates with a single word, even "Dublin" will only make sense in reversal, as form indicates sense.

Conventional plot demands may decree that the narrative press on to its conclusion, the passing out of Anna Livia, but the text and the character refuse: "Where you meer I. The day. Remember!" (626.07). Looking from right to left, backwards, we can never arrive at an ending, and *Finnegans Wake* will always remain the ultimate "To be continued's tale" (626.18).

In one sense, then, plot for Joyce has become recovery. Just as Leopold Bloom will fall asleep after pondering the events of his day, with an emphasis upon the past rather than the future, so do Anna Livia and *Finnegans Wake* greet the dawning day with "mememormee!" (628.14). Despite a seemingly final "End here" (628.13), the narrative will continue along to "Finn, again!" (628.13), and the unfinished sentence which returns us to the beginning. *Ulysses* ends with a nostos, and so too does the *Wake*. As Bloom transcends 7 Eccles Street, the Earwickers transcend Chapelizod.

Vladimir Nabokov once called Joyce's novel "a formless and dull mass of phony folklore, a cold pudding of a book, a persistent snore in the next room, most aggravating to the insomniac I am."[11] Without debating Nabokov's critical judgments, ironically enough it is just such an insomniac that Joyce is looking for in a reader. Memory, as Nabokov was well aware, entails a looking back which is recovering and uncovering, and which is a key to the novel's narrative. Bound together like the various sheets in a piece of plywood, each of the levels of plot and time segments of character can and should be understood on its own terms, and then cemented together with the others. Leopold Bloom ended up as a black dot or a full stop, but there is no period following Anna Livia's "the," and the circle of memory remains unbroken. In regard to narrative, we might ask, along with the Mamalujo, "as we there are where are we are we there?" (260.01).

Whereas a conventional novelist might be most concerned with the *result* of the plot, Joyce concentrates upon the potentiality of plot and characterization as they unfold on many levels at once. The events or the narrative levels of *Finnegans Wake* are not connected causally, but they are controlled novelistically. They are not psychoanalytic free associations, but instead they are distorted mirror reflections of each other.

Despite the fact that Joyce may be the most radical experimenter with prose fiction that the genre has ever known, he remains at heart something of a traditionalist. He simply stands the horizontal on its head to make it vertical. Rightly or wrongly, he hoped and expected that *Finnegans Wake* was a book which could be read by everybody, and his letters to Harriet Shaw Weaver, as is well known, are full of explications and helpful hints. In 1926, he asked her, "Will you let me know whether the 'plot' begins to emerge from it at all?"[12]

Most indications are that Joyce did think of the *Wake* in terms of a narrative—not necessarily one thing after another—but plot just the same. As Frank Budgen explains, "My opinion is that he did not wish to be a revolutionary originator at all. He was very conscious that he was bringing new wine to the art of the narrator, but had no intention other than to pour it on the altars of ancient tradition."[13]

In this new sense, narrative functions essentially as exposition of character, deriving from looking backward and from possibility, rather than from logicality or necessity. If HCE and ALP can best be understood as concepts or as sigla (symbols), as Roland McHugh has asserted,[14] then these overlaid, separate yet simultaneous vignettes or plot levels serve to present the m and the Δ in potential, with only a clouded glance at fictional reality. If, finally, by the reader's moving in reverse, these levels can be isolated and synthesized, and then wrapped cable-like together, the design of the narrative becomes clearer, as do our conceptions of the characters.

An examination of the multiple reports or descriptions of any event will never allow a reader to choose a "correct" one but will instead, when all are taken together, enlarge our perceptions of Wakean sin and guilt, joy and satisfaction. By turning back to memory or peering over a character's shoulder, we can rearrange what at first seemed a jumble. Whether ultimately successful or not, Joyce feels that a single, conventional narrative level would limit the artist's freedom of action, and this is his alternative to goahead plot.

4

Thy Oldworld Tales
of Homespinning and Derringdo

(431.31)

One of the basic assertions of this study is that *Finnegans Wake* does have a plot, it does tell a story, if only a reader can bring new critical perspectives to bear upon the text. Certainly a critic like Margot Norris would not agree with this statement, since she feels that "only by abandoning the novelistic approach to *Finnegans Wake* can readers free themselves from waking conventions and logic enough to enjoy the wholly imaginative reality of a dream-work."[1] Yet there still remains a novelistic form and structure behind or below the complications of the novel's primary linguistic level. Joyce, to a great degree, continues to use fairly realistic plot description—that is, at least individual incidents or sections do have a certain logic, cause and effect, a beginning, middle, and end—which can be readily perceived. The basic plot of *Finnegans Wake* is a level of narration which is interlaid, or sandwiched in, among several other levels.

In brief, the somewhat mundane actions of the Earwicker family unfold thusly: II.1, the children are outside in the yard, playing a game after school until their parents call them in at dusk for supper; II.2, after dinner, Shem and Shaun do their homework, while Issy sits on a couch, knitting and kibitzing; II.3, Earwicker presides in his pub until closing time, finishes off the drinks left around by the patrons, falls down drunk, and staggers up to bed later; III.4; The Earwickers are awakened by the cries of Shem in the throes of a nightmare, and they soothe him, return to bed, make love, and once again fall asleep as dawn is breaking; IV.1, Anna Livia

51

awakens, and her thoughts form the monologue which concludes the book. This may not be very much, as Joycean narratives never are, but, as Robert Frost said, "For once, then, something."

Finnegans Wake sometimes does tell a story on this one level, but it is also operating on several other levels simultaneously, moving from one to another with effortless ease, and leaving a reader in boundless confusion unless he or she recognizes the technique. Joyce has done away with transitions. In a conventional novel, time and space are limited; here all the potentialities of time and space are present at the same instant.

The narrative technique of the *Wake* is quite similar to that demonstrated in the Circe chapter of *Ulysses*. There Leopold Bloom has absolutely no control as a character over what is happening to him, as the bounds of time and space disappear. There are two Blooms, at least: the one we see and the one who exists in the whorehouse on another fictional level. Both exist simultaneously. Bloom can be a young boy explaining how he tore his trousers, or the Lord Mayor of Dublin, or a woman giving birth, or a prostitute being put on show for the benefit of potential customers.

As readers, we know that there is a literal narrative somewhere behind all of this: Bloom enters Nighttown looking for Stephen Dedalus, finds him at Bella Cohen's, helps him through some scrapes and some problems, and eventually gets him to the cabman's shelter. This literal narrative, however, exists in great part invisibly, in the reader's suppositions, behind the multiplicity of potentiality which Joyce is presenting as Bloom's character is dramatized and revealed. What happens is less important than what could possibly happen.

Conventional time is supplanted by the illogical logic of association. As Bloom banters on the street with the prostitute Zoe, "The mouth can be better engaged than with a cylinder of rank weed," she calls on him to "Go on. Make a stump speech out of it," (*Ulysses,* 390.1353). Suddenly this level, already once removed from fictional reality, dissolves; Bloom is elected Lord Mayor, proclaims the new Bloomusalem in the Nova Hibernia of the future, falls, becomes the womanly man, gives birth to eight coin of the realm children, and is finally eulogized by the Daughters of Erin.

Twenty-one pages later, not a second has been lost, as Zoe continues: "Talk away till you're black in the face,"[3] (*Ulysses,* 407.1958) and the narrative resumes on its previous level. Joyce has taken the reader on a quick trip through Bloom's psyche, without Poldy's permission or awareness, and has then set him back again on course. The shifting levels of reality, or of possibility, fluctuate in Circe in much the same way as they do in the Mime of Mick, Nick, and the Maggies, or anywhere else in *Finnegans Wake.* The trick is to keep them straight as one segment or episode follows another. To paraphrase Beckett, the novel is not *about* the characters: it *is* the characters.

For quite some time now we have been aware of the Joycean technique of strings of identification which broaden the scope and significance of individual characters. In this context, Shem is Shem, but he is also Satan, Cain, Jacob, the Archdruid Berkeley, the Gracehoper, James Joyce, and many others. One glance at Adaline Glasheen's "Who Is Who When Everybody Is Somebody Else"[2] should make this perfectly clear. Another characteristic which makes the narrative difficult to deal with, however, is Joyce's collapsing and expanding of the time levels on which the members of the Earwicker family perform. To say that any individual fall from grace is all falls from grace is one thing, but to explain or to understand how Shem can be a young boy playing a children's game at one moment, a Joycean-Wildean artist writing a novel at the next, and a child once more immediately afterward, is something else again.

The aforementioned symbol of the telescope might prove to be of some help here. Joyce is not interested in time as development, as in a *Bildungsroman,* but rather he examines and plays with time as immediate and simultaneous. The macrocosm and the microcosm are one, just as the various potentialities of each one of the Earwickers form a unity of characterization. At one point, Shaun describes Shem, and thus himself as well, as fifteen years old—"my leperd brethern, the Puer, ens innocens of but fifteen primes"

(483.20)—but the technique of time telescoping allows Joyce to make the twins any age he wishes at any given moment. There is no need then for linear or historical development, and the reader must adjust to each new twist of time's tail (or tale).

Interestingly enough, such time telescoping takes place only when the Earwicker children are present and when the narrative has begun to surge up close to something of a fictionally realistic level. Humphrey Chimpden and Anna Livia, adult already, are never transformed into children, though their youths may be recalled in reminiscence or flashback. Virtually all of the other characters, like Mamalujo, Kate the Slops, and the Man of All Work, remain the same. For Joyce, it appears that the adults have reached their character potential, have played out their strings, and are no longer in a state of becoming. Characters within the fables or the interpolated tales also never seem to fall into Joyce's time tunnels. The reason for this latter situation would seem to be that these fable characters exist on a level separate from the Earwickers, a level several steps below the quasi-realistic. Entities like the Mookse, the Ondt, and the Prankquean are in actuality parts of the strings of identification, and they serve to relate the Earwickers to the general and the archetypal. The time telescopings operate on a personal and specific level, amplifying the nature of an individual character.

In the middle of the novel, we are given two definitions which may help to clarify these complications of technique. For archetype, there is "we are recurrently meeting em . . . in cycloannalism, from space to space, time after time, in various phases of scripture as in various poses of sepulture" (254.24). But with the natures of the Earwickers, it is the simultaneity of time which is primary: "the allriddle of it? That that is allruddy with us, ahead of schedule, which already is plan accomplished from and syne" (274.02).

The time transformations are immediately apparent with Shem, Shaun, and Issy in the Mime. Intent upon guessing the answer to a riddle in a children's game which may also involve the color of a girl's underpants, Shem is a frustrated youngster who decides that the entire world is against him—"What's my muffinstuffinaches for these times?" (225.11). He is jeered by the Flora Girls, and Issy seems completely disgusted with her brother. "It's driving her daft like he's so dumnb. If he'd lonely talk instead of only gawk as thought yateman hat stuck hits stick althrough his spokes and if he woold nut wolly so! Hee. Speak, sweety bird!" (225.17). Shem can find no consolation. "They're all odds against him, the beasties" (227.27). "Childhood's age being aye the shameleast" (227.34), he takes out his frustrations by striking out at the nearest of his tormentors. "He dove his head into Wat Murrey, gave Stewart Ryall a puck on the plexus, wrestled a hurry-come-union with the Gillie Beg, wiped all his sinses, martial and menial, out of Shrove Sunday MacFearsome" (227.29). At a total loss as to what to do next, he decides that the only way out is to run away from home, to be a missionary, or a hedge priest, or perhaps even a writer in "Pencylmania, Bretish Armerica" (228.19). Whatever the case, he has decided once and for all that he is leaving. "He would split. He do big squeal like holy Trichepatte. . . . Byebye, Brassolis, I'm breaving!" (228.05).

At this point, however, the childish pose is abandoned, and the narrative broadens so that in his projected dreams of exile Shem becomes a grown man whose career proves to be almost a carbon copy of that of James Joyce himself. Like Oscar Wilde and John Mitchel, he would "fire off, gheol ghironal, foull subustioned mullmud, his farced epistol to the hibruws" (228.32) and "go in for scribenery with the satiety of arthurs" (229.07). His works will range from the chapter titles of *Ulysses* (229.13–16) to the overseeing of the essays of *Our Exagmination,* his introduction to *Work in Progresss:* "For he would himself deal a treatment as might be trusted in anticipation of his inculmination unto fructification for the major operation" (232.08).

Obviously for Joyce, at this moment *Finnegans Wake* was "the major operation." As the child Shem vanishes for a time, the artist asserts, "He would jused sit it all write down just as he would jused set it up all writhefully rate in blotch and void" (229.26), a drink or two ("jused") helping him to create "a most moraculous jeeremyhead sindbook for all the peoples" (229.31). He will tell how he was betrayed by all of his friends, and he will reject the twin traps of politics and religion, just as Stephen Dedalus attempted to fly the nets of Ireland: "he could neither swuck in nonneither swimp in the flood of cecialism and the best and schortest way of blacking out a caughtalock of all the sorrors of Sexton" (230.08). Even further, he boasts that he has the strength to transcend the pangs of homesickness—"forforget, forforgetting his birdsplace"— though he will accomplish this emotional feat through an esoteric rite of exorcism: "By a prayer? No, that comes later. By contrite attrition? Nay, that we passed. Mid esercizism? So is richt" (231.21). Shem as accomplished adult, however, will not remain so for long.

As in Circe, the character seems to have stepped out of the narrative and to be existing somewhere beyond it, but a message from Issy, "A claribel cumbeck to errind" (232.16), snaps things back into place. Shem returns to the fray a boy once again, after a thorough tongue-lashing from his sister: "You supposed to be the on conditiously rejected? Satanly, lade! Can that sobstuff, whingewilly! Stop up, mavrone, and sit in my lap, Pepette, though I'd much rather not" (232.22). Without a pause or a hitch, Shem is back in the game. These character oscillations serve to present Shem as a unity, as an achieved potentiality, and they describe Shem as child and adult at one and the same time. Not confined only to this single episode, these age stretchings occur over and over again throughout the *Wake*.

The same sort of temporal expansion and contraction, jumping ahead and then looking back, involves Issy as well as Shem in the Mime, but she seems more aware—if not in control—of it. Along with all her childish prattling, Issy is also described by the narrator as a flirtatious woman. "If you nude her in her prime . . . she'll prick you where you're proudest with her unsatt speagle eye. Look sharp, she's signalling from among the asters" (248.03). In the following paragraph, Issy speaks as temptress or seductress, and she seems to imply that, not only does she understand the telescope trick (as Shem does not), but she can also make sense out of it and use it to her own advantage. "I see through your weapon"

(248.15). She rues the fact that young Shem is as inept a riddle guesser as older Shem would be as a lover, but she finds the time transitions fascinating: "when he bettles backwards, ain't I fly? Pull the boughpee to see how we sleep" (248.18). (An aside to the controlling narrator: make us children again with our nursery rhymes, so that we can appear charmingly asleep in bed.) Again, "here who adolls me [adores me, turns me once more into a child] influxes sleep. But if this could see with its backsight he'd be the grand old greeneyed lobster. He's my first viewmarc since Valentine. Wink's the winning word" (249.01).

If Shem could look back now and see me, if he could see my behind, he would be as lustful and jealous as his father and could probably take his place. Certainly there are Tristan-Mark-Isolde echoes here too, but her immediate focus is on Shem, her fellow telescoper: "My belly swain's a twalf whulerusspower" (248.21). She will wink and play this game because it is fun. What she and the narrator know will not hurt anyone else. Through the telescoping, she can see "where there's a hitch, a head of things" (248.14).

To expand upon the dramatic metaphor discussed previously, the interaction of the characters and the plots in the *Wake* finds parallels in a play like Luigi Pirandello's *Six Characters in Search of an Author* or a recent film like Woody Allen's *The Purple Rose of Cairo*, where actors in a movie within a movie become involved in the viewer's lives. James Joyce could, in this light, be taken as the producer, while the narrator or narrative voice is the director. Joyce controls the director, who in turn places the Earwicker actors where he wishes them to perform. Problems arise when the players do not always agree with their roles or their dialogue, and they decide that they want to do something different or redirect the course of the drama. An actor will not always give up his or her selfhood to the persona assigned. Issy, along with all of the other characters, is self-consciously aware of her role, and she will gleefully make this fact known to the audience—to us, her readers. We are all supposed to be in on the joke, and a character often has no compunction about wandering off the stage, settling into a front row seat, and reviewing *Finnegans Wake* as it has proceeded up to that point. You can take the actor out of the masque, but you cannot always take the mask away from the actor.

If it is imperative that the reader be attuned to the shifting ages of the Earwicker children, it is equally important that we be just a bit suspicious of any new face which suddenly appears. Disguise and deception run rampant throughout the *Wake,* and the score-card which we need to tell the players apart is often only to be found by turning back to analogues which have come before. In III.2, for example, when Shaun transmogrified as Jaun prepares to take his leave of Issy, he cautions her to be chaste in his absence, and he goes to great lengths to lecture her on the perils of the pleasures of the flesh.

Though the action takes place on one level removed from a directly recognizable Earwicker interlude, it is clear that Jaun is Shaun in his threats in this chapter: "we'll dumb well soon show him what the Shaun way is like how we'll go a long way towards breaking his outsider's face for him for making up to you" (442.21). The girl here is undeniably Issy: "We. We. Issy done that, I confesh!" (459.06). Shem at first seems not to be present, but Jaun especially warns Issy against a notorious womanizer with a strange name whose features the reader may find more than a little bit familiar. "Rollo the Gunger, son of a wants a flurewaltzer . . . well over or about fifty-six or so . . . not in the studbook by a long stortch, with a toothbrush moustache and jawcrockeries . . . and of course no beard . . . cigarette in his holder . . . blueygreen eyes a bit scummy developing a series of angry boils with certain refer-ences to the Deity, seeking relief in alcohol" (443.21). This portrait certainly recalls the Shem-Joyce whom we saw in the Mime, no doubt a despicable fellow who is not to be trusted, but Jaun is not alerted, and he decides upon an even stranger precaution.

He will provide an escort and a companion for Issy who will be her protector while he is away. "I'm leaving my darling proxy behind for your consolering, lost Dave the Dancekerl, a squamous runaway and a dear old man pal of mine too" (462.16). Curiously imperceptive about this scaly snake in the grass, Jaun takes pains to emphasize the similarities of the two: "he's the sneaking likeness of us, faith, me altar's ego in miniature" (463.06); "got by the one goat, suckled by the same nanna, one twitch, one nature makes us oldworld kin. We're as thick and thin now as two tubular jawballs. I hate him about his patent henesy, plasfh it, yet am I amorist. I love him" (463.15). Again, "we're the closest of chems" (464.03); "he's very thoughtful and sympatrico that way is Brother Intellgentius, when he's not absintheminded, with his Paris addresse! He is, really" (464.16).

Despite Jaun's confidence, of course, Dave is not to be trusted, and he is yet another disguised alter ego of the other, of the opponent. If Dave is a kerl, or a churl, or a villain, he is also a dancer like Joyce at his birthday parties and like Rollo the "flure-waltzer." Dave is a "runaway," just as Shem was in the Mime. If Shem and Joyce are writers, so too is Dave: "the mightiest pen-umbrella I ever flourished on" (462.20); "he has novel ideas I know" (463.12). Shem and Issy enjoyed nursery rhymes in the Mime, and Dave becomes "yunker doodler waked to wall awriting off his phoney" (464.21). Poor Jaun inadvertently comes close to the identity of his trusted proxy, but he never does recognize the true name of his friend, "abcedminded" (18.17), who sat in Paris, "absintheminded," drinking "with his blackguarded eye and the goatsbeard in his buttinghole of Shemuel Tulliver" (464.12). Unfortunately for him, Jaun-Shaun is the naive Lemuel Gulliver who takes everything he sees at face value. Shem-Swift is the satirist, who has skillfully rearranged his role in the drama.

What follows is one of the most sexually explicit sections of *Finnegans Wake*. Since Dave speaks not a single word throughout the episode, it is difficult to be sure on what level this Shaunian escapade is actually taking place. It is not simply a fantasy, but certainly the scene is in all probability little more than voyeuristic wish fulfillment with a twist. In the Circe chapter of *Ulysses*, in a dramatization of Leopold Bloom's most deeply repressed sexual fantasy, the cuckold serves as a butler admitting Blazes Boylan into 7 Eccles Street, while his horns make do as a hat rack for the suitor's topper. Peering through the keyhole of the bedroom door,

Bloom becomes so excited that he urges the lovers on with aban-
don. "Show! Hide! Show! Plough her! More! Shoot!" (*Ulysses,*
462.3815). In much the same Peeping Tom-ish fashion, Jaun
throws his two lovers together and then encourages and coaches
the pair as if he were an overly enthusiastic fan at a football match.
"This is me aunt Julia Bride, your honour, dying to have you
languish to scandal in her bosky old delltangle. You don't reck-
oneyes him? . . . That's his penals. . . . Have a hug! . . . It's good
for her bilabials, you understand" (465.01). Jaun's commands
continue in rapidfire succession. "Be ownkind. Be kithkinish. Be
bloodysibby. Be irish. Be inish. Be offalia. Be hamlet. Be the
property plot. Be Yorick and Lankystare. Be cool. Be mack-
inamucks of yourselves. Be finish" (465.31). If anyone is guilty of
not recognizing who is who and what is going on it is Jaun, who
notes a familial parallel before he careens on to an almost Bloomian
climax: "Why, they might be Babau and Momie! Yipyip!. . . . Can
you reverse positions? . . Shuck her! Let him! What he's good for.
Shuck her more! Let him again! All she wants!" (466.01).

Jaun is aware that he is creating the fantasy—"Put me down for
all ringside seats. I can feel you being corrupted" (466.06)—but he
is never cognizant that he is directing his own defeat. As the
episode winds down, Jaun dubs Dave, "Mr Jinglejoys" (466.18),
and the reader notes that behind the many disguises of Mr. Jingle
in Charles Dickens's *The Pickwick Papers* hides James Joyce, with a
jingle of Blazes Boylan thrown in for good measure. In his heavy-
handed attempt to control the characters in their entirety, Jaun
continues to fill in Dave's background with information which
certifies Dave to us as the antagonist who succeeds by bowing to
Jaun's authority, just as Brer Rabbit manipulated Brer Fox and the
Tar Baby. Jaun cannot see, and he admits that "it's all deafman's
duff to me" (467.17). Like Joyce escaping from the Berlitz school
in Trieste and beginning work on the *Wake,* Dave is "thinking
himself into the fourth dimension . . . after he was capped out of
beurlads scoel for the sin against the past participle" (467.22).

He may be an "illstarred punster" (467.29), but he is not be-
deviled with Jaun's shortness of sight: "my seeing is onbelieving"

(468.16). Jaun rings down the curtain in triumph. "Echo, read ending! Siparioramoci! [*sipario* in Italian is "stage curtain"] . . . Well, my positively last at any stage!" (468.20). But Dave-Shem has reaped the benefits of his disguise. With extra and inside knowledge gleaned from what has already transpired within the text, the reader reads the episode one way, while Jaun-Shaun reads it in another. The face on the mask may be the face of Dave the Dancekerl, but the voice behind the mask is the voice of Shem.

Yet Shaun is not always so totally inept in his efforts to manipulate the sense and effect of the narrative, and the Saint Kevin section in Book IV is a near tribute to his deviousness. The section is framed by a question which is asked twice and answered in two totally different ways. "What does Coemghen? Tell his hidings clearly!" (602.09). "But what does Coemghem, the fostard?" (603.34). With "hidings" providing a tip-off, the two spellings of the Old Irish for Kevin delineate two separate portraits of the saint, the second the venerable and medieval Kevin who might have stepped out of the pages of Butler's or Baring-Gould's *Lives of the Saints*. "Kevin, of increate God the servant, of the Lord Creator a filial fearer" (604.27).

But the first answer concerns a mysterious Mr. Hurr Hansen appearing in a contemporary newspaper account by the reporter "Mike" Portlund, which derives directly from the present day goings-on of *Finnegans Wake*. What is the point of making Hansen yet another identity of Saint Kevin? Once again, the center of the piece is disguise and deception, and the reader must turn back to begin to solve the puzzle. Throughout the *Wake* there have been suspicions about Kevin-Shaun's sincerity, and he may have been working hard at manufacturing his own legend. "What child of a strandlooper but keepy little Kevin in the despondful surrounding of such sneezing cold would ever have trouved up on a strate that was called strete a motive for future saintity by euchring the finding of the Ardagh chalice" (110.31).

If he may have faked the recovery of the holy relic, it might be wise to take note of another previous comment by the narrator that things might not be all that they seem. "Or I will let me take it upon myself to suggest to twist the penman's tale posterwise. The gist is the gist of Shaum but the hand is the hand of Sameas. Shan - Shim - Schung. There is a strong suspicion on counterfeit Kevin and we all remember ye in childhood's reverye" (483.01). "Counterfeit" is the important word, and the Jacob-Esau deception which Shaun is trying to foist off in reverse with Kevin is confirmed by an early description of the saint: "His face is the face of a son" (602.12).

Just before the questions concerning Kevin's identity we were asked, "Was that in the air about when something is to be said for it or is it someone imparticular who will somewherise for the whole anyhow?" (602.06). It will become clear as we proceed that Kevin in particular will summarize for a string of characters in Shaun's concocted tale. Kevin stands for Mr. Hurr Hansen, who stands for the Cad with the Pipe, who stands for Shaun the Post. (We might recall that earlier Shaun was called "Hans the Curier" [125.14], the messenger who does his best to curry favor with the reader.) In an extension of yet another Shaunian dream fantasy, the reporter's lead article presents a dead Earwicker, the father overthrown at last, being celebrated at his own funeral. "Ciwareke, may he live for river" (602.21) is, of course, an anagramatized Earwicker, lying in state for "the Games funeral at Valleytemple."

Whenever reporters have popped up in the text before, the subject of their inquiries has always been HCE. "Have you evew thought, wepowtew, that sheew gweatness was his twadgedy?" (61.06); "have you ever weflected, wepowtew, that the evil what though it was willed might nevewtheless lead somehow on to good towawd the genewality?" (532.02). Further, HCE, as the Norwegian Captain, has once before been involved with the Cad and those impressive funeral games: "there was a little theogamyjig incidence that hoppy-go-jumpy Junuary morn when he colluded with the cad out on the beg amudst the fiounaregal gaames of those oathmassed fenians" (332.25). The dossier on Shaun and Mr. Hurr Hansen continues to accumulate.

Whatever effect Shaun may hope that the justification and glorification of his alter ego Saint Kevin may have upon the reader in this tale, Joyce has planted clues throughout the text which lead to a totally different interpretation. The episode is an attempt by Shaun to legitimize the projected downfall of the father by describing it as simply yet another of Kevin's miraculous accomplishments. The dawn is just breaking over Chapelizod as Shaun "but begins in feint to light his legend" (603.35). The introduction to Kevin's celebration offers a hymn of praise by the leapyear girls, who sing "by octettes ayand decadendecads by a lunary with last a lone . . . they coroll in caroll round Botany Bay. A dweam of dose innocent dirly dirls" (601.14). The "last a lone" attempts to hurry us along to the last line of the novel, but the echoes of "cad" in "decadendecads" should cause us to pause and take a closer look.

The allusion to Lewis Carroll and those dear and dirty little girls recalls a description of Shaun in the Mime, who "stud theirs with himselfs mookst kevinly . . . the churchman childfather from tonsor's tuft to almonder's toes . . . a mickly dazzly eely oily with looiscurrals" (234.10). Such greasiness is reflected in the oily smile of Mr. Hurr Hansen, "with that smeoil like a grace of backoning over his egglips of the sunsoonshine" (603.01), and the saint will soon appear as "Holy Kevin with oil extremely anointed" (605.22). Earlier, Shaun had made a truly apt comment: "Oop, I never open momouth but I pack mefood in it" (437.19). Shaun constantly betrays his intentions and his disguises in Book IV with puns and allusions whose significance he does not seem to realize.

The technique of the Saint Kevin section can be termed bricolage, bits and pieces gathered from various places, most notably from the confrontation between Earwicker and the Cad with the Pipe in I.2. "Mike" Portlund's newspaper story is saturated with such allusions, which undercut the benevolence and sincerity of Hansen's solitary stroll through the Park in the reporter's account. To delineate some of the parallels: the initial clash took place "one happygogusty Ides-of-April morning" (35.03) while Hansen walked out on "his hydes of march" (603.15), with implicit Jekyll-and-Hyde duplicity. Hansen is a "steerner among stars" (602.30), and the Cad in his self-righteousness is "swift to mate errthors, stern to checkself" (36.35). The secondary headlines from Portlund's Durban Gazette proclaim, "The last of Dutch Schulds, per-humps. Pipe in Dream Cluse" (602.23), the American gangster Dutch Schultz with his pipe or his gun in his pocket and clues to look for in this dream. The Cad is first seen "carryin his overgoat under his schulder, sheepside out" (35.13), with the allusion to Schultz and the Jacob and Esau swindle.

When Earwicker was asked the time of day, he replied that "it was twelve of em sidereal and tankard time" (35.33), time told by the stars and the pubs' opening. Hansen notes, "The greek Sideral Reulthway, as it havvents, will soon be starting a smooth with its first single hastencraft" (604.12). There are several other points of comparison which could be made, but certainly by this time Hansen has been exposed as "Schoen! Shoan! Shoon the Puzt!" (603.04). Strong doubts have been cast upon Hansen's intentions as he ambles along "talking alltheways in himself of his hopes to fall in among a merryfoule of maidens happynghome from the dance" (602.31). He is indeed a counterfeit Kevin-Shaun masquerading as the saint to glorify himself and to usurp the father's place, but he will not be allowed to get away with it. The reader can laugh with the text. "Here's heering you in a guessmasque, latterman!" (603.02). The letterman has been discovered to be a red herring.

D. H. Lawrence was of the opinion that we should trust the tale and not the teller, but even such a generally reliable pronounce-ment on fiction is not quite good enough when we come face-to-face with the narrative of *Finnegans Wake*. We certainly cannot trust the teller, and if Dave the Dancekerl and Saint Kevin are good measuring sticks we cannot really trust the tale—or at least its surface—and ultimately the reader can only rely on himself or herself. This is not to say that any interpretation of the fictional events will do, in a reader-response sort of way, but only to point out that the reader is responsible for keeping fully in mind every-thing and anything which has already occurred.

What seems requisite is an encyclopedic mind. The Saint Kevin section will make little sense without the corollary of the Ear-wicker-and-Cad-meeting subtext. Each page demands the active participation of the reader in identifying analogues, separating out conflicting voices, and juggling everything together at once. When we are told, "Kevin's just a doat with his cherub cheek, chalking oghres on walls" (27.05), we also note that he is a little toad who draws scary pictures. Joyce-the-artist controls the text, and he is not out to make a fool of the reader, but the latter must be able to range forward and back if one thing is to be connected with another. As well, *Finnegans Wake* demands multiple readings before disparate elements begin to fall into place, possibly to restate the obvious, and perhaps this is what Joyce was actually implying when he tossed off the remark that the reader must devote his or her entire life to the work. With all due respect, the *Wake* has little patience with "any simple philadolphus of a fool you like to dress . . . [who] may be awfully green to one side of him and fruitfully blue on the other . . . as a boosted blasted bleating blatant bloaten blasphorous blesphorous idiot who kennot tail a bomb from a painapple when he steals one" (167.09).

From the examinations of the two interludes above, it should become clear that another complication of *Wake* narrative is that there is no one, single tale being told here. Each one of the characters has a story, or an interpretation of a story, to tell, and they will oftentimes jostle each other in their impatience at making sure that the reader hears what each considers the "truth" of the matter. In a previous century, a reader might view with sympathy and understanding an opening statement like Esther Summerson's in *Bleak House*. "I have a great deal of difficulty in beginning to write my portion of these pages, for I know I am not clever. I always knew that. I can remember, when I was a very little girl indeed, I used to say to my doll, when we were alone together, 'Now, Dolly, I am not clever, you know very well, and you must be patient with me, like a dear.'"[3]

In the *Wake,* however, such cute sincerity would have to be taken as sly coyness instead, and the doll would begin to talk back. The Earwicker characters are not necessarily our adversaries, but they *are* clever, and there can be no bond of trust between reader and narrational voice, nor any suspension of disbelief. Each has a brief, and each is completely aware that he or she is playing to an

audience. Thus, "in this scherzarade of one's thousand one night-
inesses that sword of certainty which would indentifide the body
never falls" (51.04). Tale is piled upon tale, disguise upon disguise,
but "if you are looking for the bilder deep your ear on the
movietone" (62.08). If we are especially careful in examining the
text, we can see and hear that something recognizable which will
reveal the identity of the builder and the bilker.

We can be fairly certain that Joyce was a reader of *The Life and
Opinions of Tristram Shandy, Gentleman,*[4] and, if so, he could not
have failed to remark an aside like this: "the machinery of my work
is of a species by itself; two contrary motions are introduced into it,
and reconciled, which were thought to be at variance with each
other. In a word, my work is digressive, and it is progressive too,—
and at the same time."[5] Several commentators have noticed the
resemblances in the two works, and recently Patrick A. McCarthy
remarked, "One thing is clear: no book since *Tristram Shandy*
demonstrates its author's concern with tricking, manipulating, and
toying with its readers so incessantly as *Finnegans Wake.*"[6] The
Wake is digressively progressive in that each character, along with
the narrator, expands outwardly upon the narrative line as he or she
feels the need to amplify what has already been stated. Each reitera-
tion of an archetypal event does not supersede or correct what has
been recounted previously, but instead it offers yet another circum-
ference of possibility, along with multiple point of view. To allude
to *Tristram Shandy* just one more time for now:

> when a man sits down to write a history,—tho' it be but the history
> of *Jack Hickathrift* or *Tom Thumb,* he knows no more than his heels
> what lets and confounded hinderances he is to meet with in his
> way,—or what a dance he may be led, by one excursion or another,
> before all is over. Could a historiographer drive on his history, as a
> muleteer drives on his mule,—straight forward;—for instance, from
> *Rome* all the way to *Loretto*—without ever once turning his head
> aside either to the right hand or to the left,—he might venture to
> foretell you to an hour when he should get to his journey's end;—
> but the thing is, morally speaking, impossible: For, if he is a man of

the least spirit, he will have fifty deviations from a straight line to make with this or that party as he goes along, which he can no ways avoid. He will have views and prospects to himself perpetually solliciting his eye, which he can no more help standing still to look at than he can fly; he will moreover have various
Accounts to reconcile:
Anecdotes to pick up:
Inscriptions to make out:
Stories to weave in:
Traditions to sift:
Personages to call upon:
Panegyricks to paste up at this door.[7]

It would be hard to find a more apt description of *Finnegans Wake,* complete with sentences which attempt to run on to the horizon. Like Sterne's historian, Joyce's characters try to move in a straight line—"riding lapsaddlelonglegs up the oakses staircase on muleback" (498.03)—but there are too many accounts to reconcile and too many stories to weave in. Each Wakean digression or additional tale may seem on the surface "like another tellmastory repeating yourself" (397.07), yet each in fact enriches the texture of the character whose personality is being revealed.

Finnegans Wake's characters have been granted an autonomy which is unprecedented in modern fiction. They are able to move within the text and occasionally to step outside of it, almost at will. Yet no matter how much they cajole, or insist, or hide behind an almost endless series of personae, by their lights shall we know them. Paradoxically enough, no matter how many times they offer us yet another new face, the more are they revealed as the same old characters with the same old vested interests we knew before. To a very large extent, character in this novel is fixed. These personages do not look forward to what they may become in the future, but rather they look back to justify what they have been in the past. This is not to imply that the digressions and repetitions are boring or beside the point, for they are not. Each new-old tale expands upon the verticality of a Shem or a Shaun, demonstrating that the fascination of character lies perhaps not so much in the entity itself as in the many interpretations of such an entity.

If Marcel Proust was intent in his work upon the recapturing of lost time, Joyce is presenting characters who wish to be both what they are and were, and what they might have been. If such a feat is impossible in the cold light of day, it still remains a possibility in a dreamlike state or on an expedition into the subconscious. The pleasure lies in the journey, as Laurence Sterne would have it, rather than in the distance from Rome to Loretto or from Saint Stephen's Green to Chapelizod.

5

These Tales Which Reliterately Whisked Off Our Heart So Narrated by Thou

(431.32)

Perhaps the most vexing question of current *Wake* scholarship is the problem of voice in the novel. The basic dilemma concerns the uncovering of just who or what is speaking at any given moment and just what is being said. As Clive Hart has noted, "The difficulties are many, including not only the book's notorious density of reference and multiplicity of linguistic signs, but also its confusingly, disturbingly mixed tone. We hear many voices without knowing which, if any, to believe."[1] In one sense we may have a tendency to believe them all, since there is ultimately no right or wrong in Joyce's novel—Shaun believes he is right, as much as does Shem—but the problem of their identification remains. It is my contention that there are characters in the *Wake* who do speak and who are recognizable, whether they be the voices of the Earwickers or of the assumed identities they take on in the various fable sections of the narrative,[2] but the most complicated and confusing of them all is the narrative voice, the voice which showcases the characters and dominates the narration of the novel.

Over and over again, we are tantalized by an entity which challenges, "Listen, listen! I am doing it. Hear more to those voices! Always I am hearing them. Horsehem coughs enough. Annshe lispes privily" (571.25). Listening alone, however, will not be enough. The chameleonlike nature of the narrative voice demands that we look, as well as listen, that we hear an individual intonation while at the same time we recognize the telltale initial letters of HCE and ALP—if indeed there is such a thing as an individual intonation for the narrator. "Here keen again and begin again to make soundsense and sensesound kin again" (121.14).

To begin with, it is important to realize that the narrator is not, strictly speaking, a character in the book. Though the Earwickers are locked into their own situations and relationships, the narrator is free to move in and out of any narrational context. His voice is, and is not, a part of what we have been calling fictional reality. We may speak about the voices of Shem, or Anna Livia, or Issy, and assert that any given speech or comment of theirs has a fictionalized human referent, but the narrative voice is a different and more slippery thing. It is virtually pure style. A reader needs to become acclimatized to this self-creating, parodic voice, and one way to do this is to return briefly to the stylistic and narrational pyrotechnics of *Ulysses*.

The overlying narrational technique of *Finnegans Wake* does not spring full-blown (or Bloomed) out of Joyce's forehead; it is an extension and progression from what the artist has written before. Who writes the headlines in the Aeolus chapter? In Cyclops, the voice of an unnamed Dublin bar lounger is balanced by another voice which periodically intrudes to continue the description of the action in different parodic styles whenever and however it may wish. In actuality, since there are, by my count, thirty-two of these interpolations, there are thirty-two variations of voice. Also, though it may at first seem that the intrusions are random in terms of when and where they occur, their content and their style relate directly to the events which have just been described. Thus, for example, the parody of occultism which begins, "In the darkness spirit hands were felt to flutter (*Ulysses*, 247.338), is triggered by the amusing argument between Alf Bergan and Joe Hynes over whether Paddy Dignam is really dead. The Dubliner's sarcastic comment about Bloom, "Gob, he'd have a soft hand under a hen," gives rise to an Irish parody of what almost seems to be Dick and Jane, "Ga Ga Gara. Klook Klook Klook. Black Liz is our hen. She lays eggs for us. When she lays her egg she is so glad. Gara. Klook Klook Klook. Then comes good uncle Leo. He puts his hand under black Liz and takes her fresh egg. Ga ga ga ga Gara. Klook

Klook Klook" (*Ulysses*, 259.845). There is an internal logic to the appearance of a specific parody at any specific point.

One major effect of this kind of narration is that it sets up a dialogue between the narrational voice and the reader which exists above the consciousnesses of the characters. The various choices of style and vocabulary impart information or nuance to the reader which a realistic narrative or a goahead plot cannot supply. The context colors the voice so that the voice becomes simply a prose style, not reducible to a single character, position, or even point of view. Examining *Ulysses*, Hugh Kenner says that Joyce's "fictions tend not to have a detached narrator, though they seem to have. His words are in such delicate equilibrium, like the components of a sensitive piece of apparatus, that they detect the gravitational field of the nearest person."[3] Identifying what he calls the Uncle Charles Principle, Kenner defends Joyce's choice of the verb "repaired" to describe the venerable gentleman's progress to the outhouse in *A Portrait of the Artist* as the word which Uncle Charles himself would use.

Kenner finds the same linguistic tinting at work in *Dubliners* with Lily the caretaker's daughter in "The Dead" and Mrs. Mooney in "The Boarding House." (To add an instance of my own, the omniscient narrator in "The Boarding House" uses Jack Mooney's own language to present him as "when he met his friends he had always a good one to tell them and he was always sure to be on to a good thing—that is to say, a likely horse or a likely *artiste*. He was also handy with the mits and sang comic songs."[4] As Kenner continues, "This is apparently something new in fiction, the normally neutral narrative vocabulary pervaded by a little cloud of idioms which a character might use if he were managing the narrative."[5] It should come as no surprise that this same Uncle Charles, or perhaps Aunt Anna, Principle carries over into *Finnegans Wake*.

As a prelude, before attempting to come to grips with the narrator, it should be noted that character voices as well can be tinged by their context or by the subject they are intent upon. As we saw earlier, Shem, as MERCIUS, begins his defense of himself with something of a Shakespearean cadence. *"Domine vopiscus!* My fault, his fault, a kingship through a fault! Pariah, cannibal Cain, I who oathily foreswore the womb that bore you and the paps I sometimes sucked" (193.31). As he concludes with a tribute to his mother, however, such stylized literary language disappears, and it is replaced by the flowing style of Anna Livia herself: "little oldfashioned mummy, little wonderful mummy, ducking under bridges, bellhopping the weirs, dodging by a bit of bog, rapidshooting round the bends, by Tallaght's green hills and the pools of the phooka and a place they call it Blessington and slipping sly by Sallynoggin, as happy as the day is wet, babbling, bubbling, chattering to herself" (194.32). This seems to happen almost without Shem's knowing or intending it.

Previously, in the same chapter, when Shaun as JUSTIUS has a little trouble finding just the right epithet to condemn his brother, he consciously reverts to the latter's own language for the *mot juste.* "Shemming amid everyone's repressed laughter to conceal your scatchophily by mating, like a thoroughpaste prosodite, masculine monosyllables of the same numerical mus, an Irish emigrant the wrong way out, sitting on your crooked sixpenny stile, an unfrillfrocked quackfriar, you (will you for the laugh of Scheekspair just help mine with the epithet?) semisemitic serendipitist, you (thanks, I think that describes you) Europasianised Afferyank!" (190.33).

Granted, this is not quite a proper example of the Uncle Charles Principle, but all of the characters are equally attuned to stiles and styles. As Hugh Kenner says, "The True Sentence, in Joyce's opinion, had best settle for being true to the voice that utters it, and moreover had best acknowledge that when voices commence listening to themselves they turn into styles."[6]

Probably the most salient example of stylistic borrowing—the Uncle Charles-Aunt Anna Principle, *par excellence*—can be found in the opening sentence of III.4, which runs on for a gargantuan four pages without a full stop. The chapter begins with a dialogue between two unidentifiable voices—a sleeper who would prefer to doze off once more: "What was thaas? Fog was whass? Too mult sleepth. Let sleepth" (555.01)—and a more alert pedant who demands further background on the Earwickers, "But really now whenabouts" Expatiate then how much times we live in. Yes?" (555.03). Accordingly, the narrative voice begins to expatiate. It starts out, fittingly, in the language of those old historians Mamalujo, "So, nat by night by naught by naket, in those good old lousy days gone by" (555.05), complete with their characteristic, doggerel rhymings, as in "follow me beeline and you're bumblin, esker, newcsle, saggard, crumlin" (555.14).

As the perspective focuses more closely on the twins asleep in their beds, however, the language assumes the lisping, childish accents of the children being described. Thus, Shaun-Kevin Mary, always the food lover, "irishsmiled in his milky way of cream dwibble and onage tustard and dessed tabbage" (556.18). Shem-Jerry Godolphing, the malcontent taking his medicine "furrinfrowned down his wrinkly waste of methylated spirits, ick, and lemoncholy lees, ick, and pulverised rhubarbarorum, icky" (555.22). (The "icky" almost qualifies Shem for *Sesame Street*, but this does not mean that Joyce predicted it.) Panning across the Earwicker sleeping chambers, the narrative perspective comes across Issy, and the voice is transformed to capture her in a fitting manner: "in mauves of moss and daphnedews, how all so still she lay, neath of the whitethorn, child of tree, like some losthappy leaf, like blowing flower stilled, as fain would she anon, for soon again 'twill be, win me, woo me, wed me, ah weary me!" (555.18). Changing without warning, this narrative voice is allusive, elusive, and reflexive, picking up its accents from the fictional terrain it traverses.[7]

At least Molly Bloom's long sentences unfold in the same idiom, but, as Joyce's True Sentence continues along, it jumps to Constable Sackerson, here Wachtman Havelook Seequeerscenes, patrolling outside in the street and "stowing his bottle in a hole for at whet his whuskle" (556.26). Just as Uncle Charles would "repair," Sackerson would "stow" and "wet his whistle." As Kate the Slops recalls in dream her coming upon Earwicker earlier in the night, roused from his drunken sleep and tiptoeing upstairs, the narrative voice recounts the memory in her own inimitable phrasing: "galorybit of the sanes in hevel, there was a crick up the stirkiss and when she ruz the cankle to see, galohery, downand she went on her knees to blessersef that were knogging together like milkjuggles" (557.03). When HCE cautions her to silence, he is not overly polite and instead orders her "to whisht, you sowbelly, and the whites of his pious eyebulbs swering her to silence and coort" (557.11). Technically, all of this narration is still from the third-person, omniscient point of view, but the voice has no stylistic essence of its own. When the subject becomes the Twelve Customers, at home in their beds and dreaming of the possible causes of Earwicker's sin and guilt, their telltale, suddenly formal, "tion" constructions abound, as they speculate on "some deretane denudation with intent to excitation, caused by his retrogradation, among firearmed forces proper to this nation" (557.22).

The sentence moves to its close with a quick peek at the twenty-nine Leap Year girls musing on Shaun "with gleeful cries of what is nice toppingshaun made of made for and weeping like fun, him to be gone, for they were never happier, huhu, than when they were miserable, haha" (558.23) before ending, almost, with HCE and Anna Livia. As Albert and Victoria, rulers or reservoirs of the Nile, this final view is couched in regal language which makes them "he, Mr of our fathers, she, our moddereen ru arue rue" (558.29), but the narrative voice has one final trick to play. Throughout this entire, long section, the styles of the characters has been the subject, rather than their actions, since after all they have been doing nothing but sleeping, but the parents have begun to do *something*. The voice, however, frustrates our expectations, and will not tell us what it is: "they, ay, by the hodypoker and blazier, they are, as sure as dinny drops into the dyke. . . . A cry off" (558.30).

This True Sentence, as Kenner might call it, will only be true to its own voice, or voices, and it will not, in its own estimation, let the slightest bit of plot become a distraction here. Offering another lesson in expectation and *Wake* reading, the narrative voice may speak with others' words, but it will control what we see or do not see. Only later in this chapter will we get an inkling of what has physically begun, and the narrative voice stands indifferent to closure, perhaps momentarily satisfied with an earlier comment that "thus the unfacts, did we possess them, are too imprecisely few to warrant our certitude" (57.16). So much for goahead plot.

As a final comment on this section, it might seem at first that the stylistic perambulations might move the sentence perilously close to chaos, but this is not really the case. The sentence is divided into seven sections, and the introductions to each serve to return the reader to something of a starting point. Each of the first six is a stylistic variation of the answer to the initial question "when-abouts." It will be "when," but not quite specifically "when." It is "about." Thus, we are given the following temporal placements before each stylistic borrowing begins:

> So, nat by night by naught by naket, in those good old lousy days gone by (555.05);
> night by silentsailing night (556.01);
> nowth upon nacht (556.23);
> wan fine night and the next fine night and last find night (556.31);

> each and every juridical sessions night (557.13); niece by nice by neat by natty (558.21);

these are six introductions to style. Our flexible voice employs these tags to hold the sentence together on the one hand, while maintaining a kind of situational vagueness on the other. It is not yet time to move on with the action. The introduction to the final set piece, ALP with HCE, locates them as to "where," but not quite specifically "where": "in their bed of trial, on the bolster of hardship, by the glimmer of memory, under coverlets of cowardice" (558.26).

There seems to be a bed in the picture, a pillow, perhaps a candle or an early morning sunbeam, and some blankets, but the mysterious metaphors defy any attempt at a specific location. Why should their marriage bed be associated with trial, hardship, and cowardice, and what does memory have to do with anything? The fact that we cannot answer these questions, and indeed are not expected to, once again destroys the forward impulse and throws us back upon what we have already seen. The aforementioned sudden end of the sentence seals the matter, and we are left to contemplate the style and the voice.

The following question, "Where are we at all? and whenabouts in the name of space?" (558.33), is a kind of ricorso which brings us back again to the beginning of the True Sentence to see if we have learned anything at all. Within the narrative voice, the voices of the characters have begun to color the landscape, are carried along by a narration which includes them in almost every aspect of the storytelling.

In *Finnegans Wake*, there are two kinds of narrative voice: one which speaks to us, and one which speaks to and of itself. The first is the most easily apprehendible, for it speaks to us directly out of the pages of the novel, like Sterne's Tristram, calling for patience, urging that we do not throw down the book, and offering what it deems to be helpful hints. It seems to be our companion, draws our sympathy to itself, and becomes a fellow enjoyer, fellow sufferer. This voice puts things together, while we, the readers of Joyce, are condemned to unravel them. "I am a worker, a tombstone mason, anxious to pleace averyburies and jully glad when Christmas comes his once ayear. You are a poorjoist, unctuous to polise nopebobbies and tunnibelly soully when 'tis thime took o'er home, gin" (113.34).

The second sort of narrative voice is the voice which has just been examined in the mammoth sentence of III.4. It has no identifying marks of its own, but it draws its characteristics from whatever surrounds it. It is a style which is not committed to a particular point of view, and it becomes the quintessential spokesman for *Finnegans Wake* by incorporating all of the characters into itself without contradiction. It neither seeks nor needs a separate identity, for it is Everystyle, and it expects to be recognized by the experienced reader. Perhaps the first kind of narrative voice defines the second in this way: "So why, pray, sign anything as long as every word, letter, penstroke, paperspace is a perfect signature of its own? A true friend is known much more easily, and better into the bargain, by his personal touch, habits of full or undress, movements, response to appeals for charity than by his footwear, say" (115.06). Joyce once said to Padraic Colum, "A voice is like a woman—you respond or you do not; its appeal is direct."[8]

The narrative voice which we have seen to be so accomplished in its stylistic pirouettes in the Earwickers' dwelling has been exercising its various voices since the beginning of the book. Right from the outset, style and voice have been piled upon one another in an attempt to pierce the polished mail of the reader's mind, as a neophyte novelist like Stephen Dedalus might say. In the very first chapter, for example, the tracing of Earwicker's genealogy is begun with a formality. "Of the first was he to bare arms and a name: Wassaily Booslaeugh of Riesengeborg" (5.05), and this soon slips in tone to the jokingly familiar, "Hohohoho, Mister Finn, you're going to be Mister Finnagain! Comeday morm and, O, you're vine! Sendday's eve and, ah, you're vinegar! Hahahaha, Mister Funn, you're going to be fined again!" (5.09). The serious inquiry, "What then agentlike brought about that tragoady thundersday this municipal sin business?" (5.13), concludes with a parody of the music-hall ballad "Phil the Fluter's Ball." One tone quickly moves on to another.

Though none of the central characters has yet been officially introduced, on a second reading we can detect the accents of the Twelve and their abundance of "tion" words in "to the continuation of that celebration until Hanandhunigan's extermination!" (6.20). A Mamalujo catchphrase also pops out in the very next paragraph which follows. "So pool the begg and pass the kish for crawsake. Omen. So sigh us" (7.07). The characters and their voices are with us within the narrative voice, whether we know it yet or not. Yet again, as we proceed, a solemn description of HCE as mountain is followed by a view of ALP as river, although all of a sudden the prose becomes Anna Livia's own. "Arrah, sure, we all love little Anny Ruiny, or, we mean to say, lovelittle Anna Rayıny, when unda her brella, mid piddle med puddle, she ninnygoes nannygoes nancing by. Yoh!" (7.25).

In this first chapter the narrative voice seems to be trying out its wings, as a serious tone begins an examination of history or family, which does not work, only to move to a more playful accent, which is not successful either. It is not that the voices are out of place necessarily—the subject is wrong, since history is simply not explainable. But the narrator continues valiantly, though the reader may ask "what static babel is this, tell us" (499.34). The narrator brings to bear strategy after narrative strategy, such as the voice of Kate for a tour through the Museyroom, where even the Willingdone cannot be sure whether he is dealing with English, French, German, or Joyce. "Are we speachin d'anglas landage or are you sprakin sea Djoytsch" (485.12). The voices of Mamalujo surface for a moment—"And here now they are, the fear of um" (13.23)—for a look at the *Dublin Annals* and the colloquy between the comicstrip invaders Mutt and Jute before a new voice offers the fable of the Prankquean and Jarl van Hoother. Finally, the narrator momentarily renounces the third-person position and counters with a first-person monologue by an unnamed Irish mourner at Finnegan's wake: "Aisy now, you decent man, with your knees and lie quiet and repose your honour's lordship! Hold him here, Ezekiel Irons, and may God strengthen you! It's our warm spirits, boys, he's spooring" (27.22).

Another of Hugh Kenner's comments on *Ulysses* could also be applied here. "So, rooted in numerous realities including the multiple voices of Dublin gossip, styles proliferate and take over the Bloomsday Book: styles not arbitrarily chosen but grounded, each of them, in the texture of Bloom's experience and that of the people who experience him."[9] Multiple points of view demand multiple styles and voices, and in this first chapter the narrator is honing his narrational skills for the complexities to come, when characters emerge more fully from the text and each assumes an accent of his or her own.

There is a tendency in some *Wake* criticism to view the work as strongly autobiographical. Commentators persist in discovering James Joyce and his neuroses hiding behind Humphrey Chimpden Earwicker and his troubled and troublesome family. Margot Norris asserts that "Joyce comes to maturity when he replaces the artist's epiphany as the moment of truth with the oedipal insight into his own blindness and hypocrisy."[10] Sheldon Brivic has decided that "since association with the father is essential to resolving the oedipal complex, it seems Joyce has made progress toward health, either through the self-analysis of his work or through the experience of parenthood."[11]

It is cheering to hear that the old boy is getting better. We have seen that many joking self-portraits of Joyce dot the pages of *Finnegans Wake,* but it seems dangerous to try to make too much of them. A salient characteristic of modernism is irony. Whether or not Joyce employs his narrative voice as a disguise or as a protection remains a moot point, but the fluctuating stylistic nature of this voice results in an artistic purity, or perhaps even diffuseness, which renders autobiographical speculation fruitless. How can we know which voice is Joyce's voice? Though Joyce the artist is certainly not floating somewhere above his handiwork, paring his nails, he still should not be seen as a Dedalus at work on a diary, and, indeed, the diary voice in *A Portrait of the Artist* is not Stephen's own either—it is a style.

To locate Joyce behind all the voices is even more difficult than comprehending this precept concerning speaker, mood, and voice in II.2: "From gramma's grammar she has it that if there is a third person, mascarine, phelinine or nuder, being spoken abad it moods prosodes from a person speaking to her second which is the direct object that has been spoken to, with and at" (268.16). The narrative voice speaks to, with, and at the reader, with whatever tones that come to hand and often at the characters it is manipulating.

John Paul Riquelme confronts the problem of voice in the novel in this way: "in the *Wake,* the only definitive answer to the question '*Who is speaking?*' is the pragmatic one: the *reader* speaks by taking on the role of the artist as teller. The ambiguous status of the text's language not only allows but *requires* us to mimic the teller in different voices that merge with one another."[12] This works well if we say that the reader speaks, in a sense, by recognizing each new voice as it takes over the narration, and by realizing that these voices are the tellers. Joyce has never spoken directly to us in any of his works. The onus has always been placed upon the reader to locate the emphasis or to impart the significance.

There are many obvious cases in *A Portrait of the Artist* where the reader must supply a more insightful level of comprehension than the text supplies. We must modify Stephen's unquestioning acceptance of Mr. Casey's explanation of his crippled fingers as the result of constructing a birthday present for Queen Victoria, or Stephen's quite serious description of Dante's fury during the Christmas dinner scene: "he had heard his father say that she was a spoiled nun and that she had come out of the convent in the Alleghanies when her brother had got the money from the savages for the trinkets and the chainies. Perhaps that made her severe against Parnell."[13] (Stephen is being more than diplomatic with his polite use of "severe.") The same sort of narrational naivete was evidenced earlier in *Dubliners,* when the young boy in "Araby" comments evenly that the previous inhabitant of their house "had been a very charitable priest; in his will he had left all his money to institutions and the furniture of his house to his sister."[14] One wonders how the sister liked receiving short shrift comparable to the legacy of a second-best bed.

The reader must bring meaning to the text in yet another way. The narrative voice describes, but it does not comment. It becomes clear that the "Araby" boy, a hopeless Romantic, is confusing and intermingling romance and religion much as Emma Bovary did before him, and this thematic comment comes together in an image which the reader might tend to skip over a little too hastily. "All my senses seemed to desire to veil themselves and, feeling that I was about to slip from them, I pressed the palms of my hands together until they trembled, murmuring: *O love! O love!* many times."[15] The reader perceives what the character does not. The narrative voice is describing a supplicant with his hands clasped in a prayer to love, a symbol which encapsulates the entire tale if the reader recognizes it. As Eveline struggles to decide between running off to Buenos Aires with Frank and staying home in accordance with the sacred promise she had made to her dying mother, she looks out at the ship which could carry her to freedom. "Through the wide doors of the sheds she caught a glimpse of the black mass of the boat, lying in beside the quay wall, with illumined portholes."[16] The narrative voice seems calmly objective here, but what is the reader to make of the phrase "the black mass of the boat"? Is it possible that subconsciously Eveline regards her potential flight as a blasphemy, or is this just simple description? The reader is being called upon to make a critical judgment, and perhaps in this instance he or she takes on the role of the artist as teller.

In *Finnegans Wake*, on a basic level, the reader must decide what is a pun and what is not, what is a valid allusion in a given passage and what is not. And, going on a step further, the reader must identify voice in the *Wake* and then must ascertain whether that voice speaks truly or falsely; some voices state their positions forthrightly and some do not. The voice in "Eveline" plays its card and then leaves it there for us to interpret, but the *Wake* voice teases and plays and often is not to be trusted. We can usually rely on the narrative voice which always intends to inform, in one way or another, but the characters are a different matter.

It has become a commonplace that Shaun's first-person indictment of Shem in I.7 is to be taken with much more than a single grain of salt, and it is interesting to observe Shem's technique when their positions are reversed. Book III.1 begins with yet another of the narrator's settings of the scene. It seems to be midnight, and the parents are asleep in bed, when suddenly the narration is assumed in the first person by a voice which identifies itself as the donkey belonging to Mamalujo: "I, poor ass, am but as their fourpart tincker's dunkey" (405.06). In reality, the speaker is Shem, identified by the Shakespearean-Elizabethan inflections which punctuate his seemingly objective description of his brother. "Methought as I was dropping asleep somepart in nonland of where's please" (403.18). "Save 'twere perchance anon some glistery gleam . . . methought broadtone was heard. . . . Now, 'twas as clump, now mayhap" (403.24). As Shaun's appearance is fleshed out in this dream interlude, Shem devotes several pages to his sartorial splendor—"dressed like an earl in just the correct wear" (404.16)—but soon the imagery becomes less that of fashion and more that of the delights of the dining room table.

Where Shaun inveighed, Shem insinuates We find that Shaun's coat sports "great sealingwax buttons, a good helping bigger than the slots for them, of twentytwo carrot krasnapoppsky red" (404.23), and that R.M.D., the initials of the Dublin Royal Mail, are splashed across the garment's front "with his motto through dear life embrothred over it in peas, rice, and yeggyyolk" (404.28). Shem continues to praise the Post: "that young fellow looked the stuff, the Bel of Beaus' Walk, a prime card if ever was!" (405.13). Shaun's healthy appearance and great strength are attributed to the fact that he eats three square meals a day, plus a snack: "he had recruited his strength by meals of spadefuls of mounded food" (405.29). We might remember that Shaun does not like Shem's eating habits either. "Shem was a sham and a low sham and his lowness creeped out first via foodstuffs" (170.25). The account of Shaun's culinary itinerary continues with a rush of realistic description worthy of Theodore Dreiser's minute account of the contents of Sister Carrie's plate, punctuated with the interjection of Shaun's own call for more:

> next, the half of a pint of becon with newled googs and a segment of riceplummy padding, met of sunder suigar and some cold forsoaken steak peatrifired from the batblack night o'erflown then, without prejuice to evectuals, came along merendally his stockpot dinner of a half a pound or round steak, very rare, Blong's best from Portarlington's Butchery, with side of ricey peasy and Corkshire alla mellonge and bacon with (a little mar pliche!) a pair of chops and thrown in from the silver grid by the proprietoress of the roastery who lives on the hill (405.33).

Shem's manipulation of the narrative relies for its broad comic effect on the complicity of the reader, just as the presence behind

Stephen's voice in *A Portrait of the Artist* counted on our knowing smiles. The Shem voice will turn Shaun's own language against him, but always with a statement of its own innocence. "I don't mean to make the ingestion for the moment that he was guilbey of gulpable gluttony as regards chewable boltaballs, but, biestings be biestings" (406.32). Where Shaun relied on a rhetorical sledgehammer to make his point, Shem engages his opposite in a conversation with sympathetic sounding, leading questions, so that Shaun has more than enough rope to hang himself. Almost all of this chapter is direct dialogue, and Shem wheedles the true stance of Shaun out of him—for example, with an understanding of how hard it must be to slave away as a mailman. "Would you mind telling us, Shaun honey, beg little big moreboy, we proposed to such a dear youth, where mostly are you able to work. Ah, you might! Whimper and we shall" (410.28). Accordingly, Shaun complains of how tired and overworked he is, but he also outlines his culinary-Catholic code which enables him to get through each day. "Never back a woman you defend, never get quit of a friend on whom you depend, never make face to a foe till he's rife and never get stuck to another man's pfife. Amen, ptah! His hungry will be done! . . . I do my reasonabler's best to recite my grocery beans" 411.08).

His fable of the Ondt and the Gracehoper only serves to indict the meanness of the Ondt, and, as he becomes more and more indignant at the Shem he does not recognize standing in front of him, Shaun's charges become more and more ridiculous. Shem is a "homo!" (422.11); the supposed brothers are not actually related. Shem steals his ideas from Shaun. "Shem Skrivenitch, always cutting my prhose to please his phrase" (423.15). Even the infamous letter was plagiarized from Shaun: "He store the tale of me shur. Like yup. How's that for Shemese?"(425.02). While a reader might have a tendency to believe what Shaun says in I.7, as commentators did for years, Shem makes sure here that there will be no mistake. Fooled by a voice, Shaun is hoisted by his own petard.

Thus we may say that each of the character voices in the *Wake* has its own individual strategy which plays with the reader in a different way. The reader must be constantly on guard, ready to greet each new point of view with the challenge "well, tell it to me befair, the whole plan of campaign, in that bamboozelem mincethrill voice of yours. Let's have it, christie!" (515.27). As we have seen, Shaun will not always be fair, and he will attempt to lead the reader down the garden path with disguised pieces of plot. Shem too is a trickster, but he performs his feats of narrational sleight of hand with the full knowledge that we can see through his hoaxes and still enjoy them at the same time.

There is a touch of compassion in the Shem voice, perhaps the difference between mercy and justice, which can evaluate the Post clearly yet can still allow a touch of good will. In his final soliloquy, Shem reflects about Shaun, "how you would be thinking in your thoughts how the deepings did it all begin and how you would be scrimmaging through your scruples to collar a hold of an imperfection being committed" (428.04). But he still can wish him well, "like the good man you are, with your picture pockets turned knockside out in the rake of the rain for fresh remittances and from that till this in any case, timus tenant, may the tussocks grow quickly under your trampthickets and the daisies trip lightly over your battercops" (428.23).

Although it may not be fashionable to make value judgments about the characters in *Finnegans Wake,* there is a pronounced difference between these two voices. If nothing else, one has a sense of humor and the other definitely does not. With Shem, "the voice is the voice of jokeup, I fear" (487.21), and we might just as well sit back and enjoy it.

Despite all the critical concern with the guilty and failing Earwicker and the protective and nurturing Anna Livia, it should be noted that it is the children's voices which predominate in the text. Shaun speaks at the greatest length, followed by Shem and Issy, while the parents lag far behind. Like her brothers, Issy seems fully aware that she is being watched and listened to by the reader, as we saw with the time telescopings. Whether in her footnotes in II.2 or in her answer to the tenth question in I.6, she preens herself in the reader's mind with clothing imagery which parallels Shaun's obsession with food. "Listen, loviest! Of course it was *too* kind of you, miser, to remember my sighs in shockings, my often expressed wish when you were wandering about my trousseaurs and before I forget it don't forget, in your extensions to my personality, when knotting my remembrancetie, shoeweek will be trotting back with red heels at the end of the moon but look what the fool bought cabbage head and, as I shall answer to gracious heaven, I'll always in always remind of snappy new girters, me being always the one for charms" (144.20).

Issy and her brothers have a public and dramatic sense which their voices acknowledge; they are willing participants in a new kind of fiction in which the characters are partners in the presentation with the narrator and the reader. Issy counsels her dream lover, "Shy is him, dovey? Musforget there's an audience" (147.01), and she is quite conscious of her entrances and exits. "Of course I know you are a viry vikid girl to go in the dreemplace and at that time of the draym and it was a very wrong thing to do, even under the dark flush of night" (527.05). The younger generation is the true center of *Finnegans Wake,* and it is their voices which clamor most directly and insistently for the reader's attention.

Both Anna Livia and Humphrey Chimpden Earwicker do speak occasionally throughout these pages, but they enunciate their positions in totally different ways than do the children. HCE has only two major speeches in the entire novel (363.20 and 532.06); more often than not he is spoken about by the other characters—when he comes to their attention at all. Where the siblings are active and assertive, the father is passive and defensive. With his characteristic stammer, HCE makes only a couple of extended declarations of his innocence in regard to the incident in the Park. "I am as cleanliving as could be and that my game was a fair average since I perpetually kept my ouija wicket up. On my verawife I never was nor can afford to be guilty of crim crig con of malfeasance trespass against parson with the person of a youthful gigirl frifrif friend chirped apples" (532.16).

Strangely enough, HCE does not recognize the presence of the reader, or even of the narrator, and almost never does he even acknowledge the existence of his wife and children. The center of his focus is himself. While we come to some sense of knowing the other characters through their speeches, this shadowy figure passes through the novel unaware of anything more than his own unending guilt. "I am ever incalpable where release of prisonals is concerned of unlifting upfallen girls wherein dangered from them in thereopen out of unadulteratous bowery, with those hintering influences from an angelsexonism. It was merely my barely till their oh offs. Missaunderstaid" (363.32). To make another value judgement, HCE in person is simply not as interesting as the supporting cast which surrounds him and steals the show.

Anna Livia, too, seems cut off from the drama unfolding around her, supporting her husband but confused by the flashy twists and turns of the narrative. "Tomothy and Lorcan, the bucket Toolers, both are Timsons now they've changed their characticuls during their blackout" (617.12). Something has happened to the twins, but she does not know what. She usually speaks meditatively to herself, not to the reader, and essentially her perspective is inward, back to the past and to her recognition of the fact that she is the one who has been truly misunderstood. "But you're changing, acoolsha, you're changing from me, I can feel. Or is it me is? I'm getting mixed" (626.35). Her earlier comment, "My heart, my mother! My heart, my coming forth of darkness! They know not my heart, O coolun dearast!" (493.34) presages a later statement of ultimate frustration—"A hundred cares, a tithe of troubles and is there one who understands me? One in a thousand of years of the nights?" (627.14). It seems that the time of the parents has passed, and they flounder about in a narrational and thematic maze which only the children can travel through with ease. Where the children speak to each other and to us, the parents are resigned to monologues which, they think, only they can hear. The Viconian supplanting of the generations is demonstrated thus by full-scale communication and the lack of it.

Finnegans Wake, then, is indeed a book of talk whose voices are orchestrated by a narrator attuned to nuance. As the voice cautions, "Stick wicks in your earshells when you hear the prompter's voice"

(435.19). Rather than unfolding in a logical progression of narrative, the text is basically composed of individual segments, each self-contained as to voice or voices. The voice shifts or changes according to context, and, once a reader has ascertained the number of speaking parts, he or she can adjust to the at first seemingly chaotic nature of a tale whose point of view switches incessantly. Basically, we are in the hands of the children here, a tribe of polyglot manipulators who seem to enjoy very much what they do, who seem to enjoy the freedom which the *Wake* has given them. In their strivings with and against each other, they provide an alternative to the idea that the meek shall inherit the earth. We must keep an eye and an ear upon these mischievous miscreants, hoping along with Anna Livia that all will come clear in the end.

6

They Are Tales All Tolled

(275.24)

Soon after the Lestrygonians chapter of *Ulysses* was published in the *Little Review*, Joyce said to Frank Budgen, "I have just got a letter asking me why I don't give Bloom a rest. The writer of it wants more Stephen. But Stephen no longer interests me to the same extent. He has a shape that can't be changed."[1] The section III.3 of *Finnegans Wake* takes voice and character even further than we have seen them transformed before, and change runs rampant throughout the episode. The emergence of Yawn as the center of this chapter, after having passed through the permutations of Shaun and Jaun in previous chapters, represents a kind of stripping of characteristics from character which results in nothing more nor less than voice—until the coming of HCE. It is not that the character of Shaun has degenerated, as commentators have generally assumed, but instead his character has been drained of identifying marks and features so that he appears as little more, at last, than a mechanical transmitter. There is a voice behind the facade of Yawn, but there is no essence. As we are told in the opening paragraph, "His dream monologue was over, of cause, but his drama parapolylogic had yet to be, affact" (474.04). As Shaun, his speeches are finished, but his new dramatic appearance encompasses paralogism (faulty reasoning), polylogy (garrulousness),[2] and, given the connotations of "para" and "poly," a going beyond many or multiple logical systems. By the end, Shaun-Yawn is refined out of existence, not even allowed to be a voice crying in the Wakean wilderness.

89

If we have been treating extensively the end to goahead plot in *Finnegans Wake*, it becomes apparent that III.3 has no plot whatsoever. Once the narrator has set the scene of Yawn asleep on a hilltop, "All of asprawl he was laying too amengst the poppies and, I can tell you something more than that, drear writer, profoundly as you may bedeave to it, he was oscasleep asleep" (476.19), with Mamalujo congregating around him for an interrogation ("those four claymen clomb together to hold their sworn starchamber quiry on him" [475.18]), the remaining seventy-eight pages of the chapter are composed of direct dialogue. All that we get is voice, and what little bits of information which do occasionally float to the surface are old hat, all something that we have heard before.[3]

In many ways the chapter represents the ultimate defeat of Mamalujo and the Mamalujo method, the search for specific historical truth which can only end in failure. Thus, in answer to a question about the girls in the Park, Yawn can only come up with a reprise of the Prankquean's fable: "Peequeen ourselves, the prettiest pickles of unmatchemable mute antes I ever bopeeped at, seesaw shallsee, since the town go went gonning on Pranksome Quaine" (508.26). Earwicker is once again the Willingdone in the Museyroom: "Would that be a talltale too? This was the grandsire Orther. This was his innwhite horse. Sip?" (510.29), and once again the Norwegian Captain: "—I think you're widdershins there about the right reverence. Magraw for the Northwhiggern cupteam was wedding beastman, papers before us carry" (511.01). The analogues have ceased providing us with anything new, and this is the last time that Mamalujo will appear in the *Wake*—notwithstanding their upcoming bedpost roles—with anything at all resembling the importance they have assumed up until now.

In the Ithaca chapter of *Ulysses* the question and answer format, as convoluted and seemingly distanced as it can be at times, still leads us closer to the essences of Stephen Dedalus and Leopold Bloom. Even the concluding black dot is pregnant with meaning which locates Bloom in his relation to the cosmos and to the mythic figures which have come before him. But at this point in the development of *Finnegans Wake*, word of mouth is proving to be of no use. The Four begin as fishermen "spreading in quadriliberal their azurespotted fine attractable nets, their nansen nets, from Matt Senior to the thurrible mystagogue after him and from thence to the neighbor and that way to the puisny donkeyman and his crucifer's cauda" (477.19), but a Nansen passport will not allow free passage, and they will catch no salmon of knowledge.

The interrogators and their subject cannot even agree upon a common language for communication, and a Mamalujo comment in Latin about the incomprehensibility of all this (478) is answered by Yawn in rambling, broken French. The Four search for a common ground: "I am told by our interpreter, Hanner Esellus, that there are fully six hundred and six ragwords in your malherbal Magis landeguage" (478.08), though no Rosetta stone will be found. In reply to questions about the nature and residence of the father figure, Yawn ignores the problem and will only lament the disappearance of the girl. "For my darling. Typette! . . . For my darling dearling one. . . . Have you seen her? Typette, my tactile O! . . . Have you seen my darling one? I am sohohold!" (478.03). To make things even worse, just as they did in II.4 with the tale of Tristan and Isolde, Mamalujo cannot refrain from digressing constantly, telling irrelevant stories and reminiscing about the past. For no apparent reason, Johnny suddenly recalls the pleasures of his childhood at some length, and he asks, in a neighborly way, "Do you know my cousin, Mr Jasper Dougal that keeps the Anchor on the Mountain, the parson's son" (479.10). Nothing goes forward, and instead the issues bounce up and down like a pogo stick.

So far Yawn, still retaining some sort of constitutionality, is locatable, but he would prefer to escape all this bother in the arms of Morpheus: "Dream. Ona nonday I sleep. I dreamt of a somday. Of a wonday I shall wake. Ah!" (481.07). When he can be roused by hard and direct questioning such as "we speak of Gun, the farther. And in the locative. Bap! Bap!" (481.19), Yawn answers in tired circles and platitudes without any location: "By him it was done bapka, by me it was gone into, to whom it will beblive . . . he could be all your and my das" (481.24). Language itself is breaking down, and syntax and style are slipping away into confusion. A barely understandable question concerning the father's name, or his ears—"Breeze softly. Aures are aureas. Hau's his naun?" (482.03) provokes an ungrammatical answer about his eyes—"Me das has or oreils. Piercey, piercey, piercey, piercey!" (482.04). The stern "but where do we get off, chiseller?" is parried with a sexy stop on the bus line: "haltstille, Lucas and Dublinn! Vulva! Vulva! Vulva! Vulva!" (482.06). Obviously, things cannot go on long like this, and Mark is becoming just as aggravated and irritated as is the reader. The historian in charge will call for order—"Number four, fix up your spreadeagle and pull your weight!" (482.14)—but the echo of the washerwomen from I.8 has little effect. Though at least we got some information there, we will get little here.

Ironically, Matt can state an essential principle of *Finnegans Wake*—the presentation of paradox and the fusion of seeing and hearing—but none of the Four can put into practice what the reader is expected to grasp: "That's the point of eschatology our book of Kills reaches for now in soandso many counterpoint words. What can't be coded can be decorded if an ear aye sieze what no eye ere grieved for" (482.33). The father has passed out of the picture for now, the pursuit of knowledge about him is a blind alley, and he should be left to death, judgment, and memory. The father is fading fast, and, despite his final, extended appearance at the end of this chapter, it is the mother who will have *Finnegans Wake*'s final word.

The Four cannot even be sure to whom it is they are speaking: "I will let me take it upon myself to suggest to twist the penman's tale posterwise. The gist is the gist of Shaum but the hand is the hand of Sameas" (483.01). But, even given their justifiable suspicions, Shem is conspicuous by his absence in this chapter. It is the Post who is on the spot. Despite Yawn's avowal of his own sincerity and of his own authenticity—"What cans such wretch to say to I or how have My to doom with him?" (483.17)—his defense of "the person whomin I now am" (484.05) casts doubt on the entire notion of assignable character. The voice may be momentarily in residence in a single character at the moment, but there is no guarantee that it will remain there for long.

The Four continue to hammer away at the history of HCE: "What about your thruppenny croucher of an old fellow, me boy, through the ages, tell us, eh?" (485.17). In response, the Yawn witness retreats behind pidgin English and attempts to escape: "Me no angly mo, me speakee Yellman's lingas. . . . Me pigey savvy a singasong anothel time" (485.29). Since we only *hear* the Yawn voice, and never get to *see* what the entity looks like since there is no physical description, Joyce is free to play with character which can never be pinned down, which can be eternally mobile and malleable. In such a situation, ultimately we can no longer speak of character at all and can only locate voice by the telltale tones which we hear.

Mamalujo will go so far in their confusion as to initiate an occult ritual or seance, with a nod to Yeats and the Order of the Golden Dawn, placing the letter T to Yawn's forehead the better to plumb the depths of his subconscious. They compose a tryptich vision with three questions—"Do you see anything, templar? . . . What do you feel, liplove? . . . / What do you hear, breastplate?" (486.16)—but nothing appears but snippets of a Tristan-Isolde dream and a tag from an unsolvable Celtic riddle: "I ahear of a hopper behidin the door slappin his feet in a pool of bran" (486.30). This tripartite view which cannot compose itself stands in ironic contrast to the triple view of IV.1 which encompasses Saint Kevin, Saint Patrick and the Archdruid, and Anna Livia, and which states the significant presence and revival of the brothers and the mother. The fragments of III.3 will come together in the final chapter to describe the resurgence of character in the archetypal entities who will carry on, who will be around when "every talk has his stay" (597.19). Ultimately, the voice of Anna Livia, unique and identifiable, will bring a coherence to the *Wake* text which is lacking in the multimicrophonic colloquy of Yawn and Mamalujo.

Both parties in the interrogation seem gradually to become aware that all is not as it should be, that voice and character are metamorphosing right before their ears. The Four ask if Yawn-Shaun realizes that he "might, bar accidens, be very largely substituted in potential secession from your next life by a complemen-

tary character, voices apart." They conclude, "The voice is the voice
of jokeup, I fear. Are you imitation Roma now or Amor now"
(487.02). Yawn's reply acknowledges the fact that, in terms of
character, he is no one thing at all, and more is still to come: "I
swear my gots how that I'm not meself at all, no jolly fear, when I
realise bimiselves how becomingly I to be going to become. . . .
You knew me once but you won't know me twice" (487.17). The
concern now is not with the assembling of information in the
neverending cases of HCE's sin and the sibling rivalry, but rather
the subject momentarily becomes the method. What is this, and
how is it being told? They are not dealing with a narrative, but with
a "letter self-penned to one's other, that neverperfect everplanned"
(489.33), whose rationale can be discerned from within, but not
from without. The story is "this nonday diary, this allnights news-
eryreel" (489.35) in which the film has been spliced together to
play over and over again.

To mix metaphors, anyone can join the conversation on the
Wakean CB radio: "In this wireless age any owl rooster can peck up
bostoons" (489.36), and no one speaker can be secure and identifiable for long. As the Mamalujo conclude simply, "I get it. By
hearing his thing about a person one begins to place him for a
certain in true" (490.09). But they will soon see that listening to a
voice will allow them to place him only for a second, and definitely
not for certain.

The confidence with which they return to listening is immediately shattered by a deluge of different outbursts which all seem
to demand insistent attention. All at once an Earwicker voice leaps
in to protest his innocence: "Loonacied! Marterdyed!!" (492.05),
and this is quickly followed by Anna Livia's impassioned defense of
"my dodear devere revered mainhirr . . . my deeply forfear re-
vebereared . . . my rupee repure riputed husbandship" (492.16).
The sudden transition from voice to voice is too much for
Mamalujo to handle and throws them into consternation. Even
ALP's characteristic "my heart, my mother! My heart, my coming
forth of darkness! They know not my heart" (493.34) is not a
strong enough clue for them, and their best guess is that this might

be the Prankquean showing up yet once more: "For why do you lack a link of luck to poise a pont of perfect, peace?" (493.29). Anna Livia's final statement is couched as yet another version of the Letter, ending with "respect. S. V. P. Your wife. Amn. Anm. Amm. Ann" (495.33), but even this leaves the Four unconvinced as to her identity.

The novel is moving along, page after page, but their comprehension lags far behind since they have not grasped what they are dealing with—a fictional echo chamber with no overtly logical transitions between the voices. A voice which sounds suspiciously like Issy's reverts to childish bubbling, yet it still puts the problem into a nutshell: the interchangeability of voice. "I have it here to my fingall's ends. This liggy piggy wanted to go to the jampot. And this leggy peggy spelt pea. And theese lucky puckers played at pooping tooletom. Ma's da. Da's ma. Madas. Sadam" (496.18). Multiple personality and mutable voice result in combinations and reversals which lead to everything and nothing. To the four questioners, these speeches and this novel are only "your exagmination round his factification for incamination of a warping process" (497.02).

This preceding comment, invoking the Twelve, leads to a kind of dream vision of Earwicker once again lying in state at his wake "healed cured and embalsemate, pending a rouseruction of his bogey" (498.36), and it is significant in that again the point is underlined that the father is becoming of little consequence. There will be neither the ruction nor the resurrection that enlivened Finnegan's wake, though his bogey or spirit is still to appear. But Earwicker proves to be "most highly astounded, as it turned up, after his life overlasting, at thus being reduced to nothing" (499.01).

The Four refuse to believe that all could be up with the subject of their informational quest: "D'yu mean to sett there where y'are now . . . repeating yurself, and tell me that?" (499.19), but Yawn is adamant. If they will not accept the truth, then Yawn will see to it that all communication is disrupted by unleashing the myriad number of speakers within him: "I mean to sit here on this altknoll where you are now . . . like a sleeping top, with all that's buried ofsins insince insensed insidesofme. If I can't upset this pound of pressed ollaves I can sit up zounds of sounds upon him" (499.23). And immediately he proceeds to do so, as a cacaphony of sounds and voices reduces the conversation to total confusion. "What static babel is this, tell us?" (499.34). Unrecognizable voices intone chants of "Usque! Usque," and "Whoishe whoishe," and amid the ever popular "Zinzin. Zinzin" a welter of battles seems to erupt, and the center of comprehension will not hold: "Slog slagt and sluaghter! Rape the daughter! Choke the pope!" (500.17).

In the midst of this dissolution, the pitiful voice of Earwicker can be heard for a moment, a combination of three fallen Celts—Tristan, Jonathan Swift, and Charles Stewart Parnell—calling upon Issy for last minute help as he passes away: "Sold. I am sold! Brinabride! My ersther! My sidster! Brinabride, goodbye! Brinabride! I sold!" (500.21). Sold and old, poor Earwicker does not seem to notice the shift in her use of pronouns as youth rejects age: "Pipette dear! Us! Us! Me! Me!" (500.22). Issy is unconcerned and even blandly uninterested in the father's plight, almost gazing off into space: "—Brinabride, bet my price! Brinabride! / —My price, my precious?" (500.27). Apparently paying little attention to the gist of the conversation, the Four attempt to zero in on the transmission: "Now we're gettin it. Tune in and pick up the forain counties! Hello!" (500.35). Breaking in, they can almost identify Issy: "Hello! Tittit! Tell your title? . . . / —Hellohello! Ballymacarett! Am I thru' Iss? Miss? True?" (501.02). But her last reply ends the dialogue abruptly: "Tit! What is the ti . .? / SILENCE" (501.05).

The echo of the Cad's question asking the time of Earwicker in Phoenix Park, and perhaps the hint of a woman's breast, underline the father's guilt which he will not fully acknowledge. No matter who is responsible for the breaking off, it is clear that Earwicker has not a leg to stand on. Condemning him absolutely, Margot Norris declares that "he is uncertain of name and identity, unlocatable rather than a center that fixes, defines, and gives meaning to his cosmos. He is a lawbreaker rather than lawgiver. As head of the family, he is incestuous rather than the source of order in the relations of his lineage."[4] It is not that Earwicker is necessarily to be completely rejected, however, but only that his time is past. The unrolling of the ages demands that the elders give up their places to the young. The Sin, such as it may have been, is over and done with and best forgotten.

If we accept the proposition that this chapter is, among other things, documenting the diminution of the father's prominence, if this is to be Earwicker's last hurrah, then it is important to recognize the role that Yawn-Shaun plays in the reversal. In general Shaun is usually viewed in something of a negative light, with his lewd moralizing and seemingly unwarranted attacks upon his brother, but in III.3 he serves a truly useful function. His comments and evaluations are not so much directed toward some sort of violent overthrow of the father as they are a balanced statement of the fact that Earwicker has played a valuable part in the evolution of the archetypal pattern. But that part has reached its final stages, and Yawn-Shaun does not always see the relevance of continuing the discussion forever, as Mamalujo seem content to do. In the second section of this chapter, before he is interrupted by the other voices, Yawn-Shaun seems to agree to construct an unbiased portrait of Earwicker and his peccadilloes, to tell as much as he knows, or can remember, or can surmise about the father. Perhaps, if they are finally satisfied, Mamalujo will leave him in peace. And so, after the previous violent interruption, the scene is set once more: "Act drop. Stand by! Blinders! Curtain up. Juice, please! Foots!" (501.07). The Four have managed to reestablish radio contact: "Yes. Very good now. We are again in the magnetic field. . . . Moisten your lips for a lightning strike and begin again. Mind the flickers and dimmers! Better?" (501.15). Yawn-Shaun will soon return to the witness stand with voices in the wings waiting to correct him if he should miss a step.

After pausing briefly for Issy's account of a tremendous storm, the spotlight returns to Yawn-Shaun: "From Miss Somer's nice dream back to Mad Winthrop's delugium stramens" (502.29). Asked about how Earwicker and Anna Livia first became acquainted—"Now do you know the wellknown kikkinmidden where the illassorted first couple first met with each other?" (503.08)—Yawn-Shaun obliges with a description of a primeval scene, HCE and ALP as intertwined trees in a prelapsarian garden, "each and all of their branches meeting and shaking twisty hands all over again in their new world through the germination of its gemination" (505.10).

Despite the happy lyricism of this passage, it is inevitable that the parents should fall, that the felix culpa will involve the sexual, and that God will expel them from the Garden. Their amorous behavior was called to God's attention, and He responded as we all would expect: "Such was a bitte too thikke for the Muster of the hoose so as he called down on the Grand Precurser who coiled him a crawler of the dupest dye and thundered at him to flatch down off that erection and be aslimed of himself for the bellance of hissch leif" (506.04). Accused not only as Adam, Earwicker is accused also as the Serpent, damned from both sides at once. This is a story known to all men, and women too, and Yawn-Shaun is self-aware enough to know that the archetypal tale has been done to death: "Wo wo! Who who! Psalmtimes it grauws on me to ramble, ramble, ramble" (506.13). He has had enough already, and coyly he tries to avoid the subject of the parents by saying that their doings do not represent a moral and upright example for his listeners: "Never you mind about my mother or her hopitout. I consider if I did I would feel frightfully ashamed of admired vice" (506.32).

It is funny to observe Yawn-Shaun twist and turn as he eludes the obsessive and singleminded questioning, and he feigns innocence as the Four level charge upon charge against HCE. Curiously enough, in contrast to his previous undercutting and undermining of Earwicker in earlier appearances, Yawn-Shaun can almost be said to sympathize with the father's human frailties. When Mamalujo zero in on the Sin in the Park, Yawn-Shaun explains that the two girls involved in the case were the prettiest things to be seen around Dublin since Maud Gonne or the Prankquean, as was mentioned earlier. Perhaps HCE simply could not help himself from looking: "Peequeen ourselves the prettiest pickles of unmatchemable mute antes I ever bopeeped at, seesaw shallsee, since the town go went gonning on Pranksome Quaine" (508.26). His tribute to their beauty is so rapturous that the Four ask if he might have been in the Park as well: "And were they watching you as watcher as well?" (508.35). Yawn-Shaun answers that their assertion is simple nonsense: "Where do you get that wash? This representation does not accord with my experience. They were watching the watched watching" (509.01).

The language, the syntax and grammar, of this section are quite clear and wideawake and, when the Four ask about Yawn-Shaun's feelings about the situation, his sympathy for Earwicker peeks through even as he tries to disguise it: "But I was dung sorry for him too. / —O Schaum! Not really? Were you sorry you were mad with him then? / —When I tell you I was rooshiamarodnimad with myself altogether, so I was, for being sorry for him" (509.09). Without commiting himself completely to the father's side— "Would you blame him at all stages?"—he hedges a bit and states that customs change from place to place, and perhaps we do not know enough about the case to condemn him: "I believe in many an old stager. But what seemed sooth to a Greek summed nooth to a giantle. Who kills the cat in Cairo coaxes cocks in Gaul" (509.17). This is certainly the more pliant voice of a different Shaun with a more understanding point of view.

We may be totally surprised to hear Yawn-Shaun refuse to take a moral position on the Earwicker case, but this he does emphatically. All that can ultimately be said is that HCE is the man, the father, who, like Jarl von Hoother and the Russian General "made a piece of first perpersonal puetry that staystale remains to be. Cleaned" (509.35). While the Four search for the specific, Yawn-Shaun has opted for the broader view, looking now to the future which will include himself, and Shem, and Issy, rather than to the past. When the Four wonder if Earwicker is being reduced to an inconsequential character in a nursery rhyme—"So this was the dope that woolied the cad that kinked the ruck that noised the rape that tried the sap that hugged the mort?" (511.32)—Yawn-Shaun concurs that indeed he should be, along with the gossip, and that the entire scandal is probably someone's idea of a joke: "That legged in the hoax that joke bilked" (511.34).

The fictional house that Joyce is building has neither time nor room for moral judgments, transcends sin or blame, and asks only that the father and mother be respected for what they were, the male and female who were fated to recognize each other and come together. To Mamalujo's supposition—"He came, he kished, he conquered. . . . The most of his glancefull coaxing the beam in her eye? That musked bell of this masked ball! Annabella, Lovabella, Pullabella, yep?"—Yawn-Shaun will reply with a simple and affirmative, Mollyesque "Yup!" (512.08).

As we saw in the first part of this chapter, communication begins to break down the longer the questioning continues. The queries of Mamalujo increase in length and bulk, while Yawn-Shaun's answers get briefer and briefer. The Four never seem to get the point (and perhaps how could they?), the closer the answers get to incorporating the identities of the archetypal lovers into couples who extend beyond *Finnegans Wake*. The interrogators demand specifics, and an exasperated Yawn provides information which points above and outside the text: "Ninny, there is no hay in Eccles's hostel. / —Yet an I saw a sign of him, if you could scrape out his acquinntence? Name or redress him and we'll call it a night!" (514.15). The Four will let him off the hook and go home, if he will supply the name, but Yawn responds with the cryptic "—.i..'. .o..l." (514.18), or "Finn's Hotel," where the young Nora Barnacle was a chambermaid when she first walked out with James Joyce.

The analogues which have been offered then are Leopold and Molly Bloom ("Eccles's hostel") and James and Nora Joyce, as the text begins to fold in upon itself, self-reflexive as always. There are boxes within boxes, expanding and contracting almost at will. There is no hope that one side will ever understand the other, and Yawn-Shaun notes again that the questioning is becoming boring and repetitive: "Which? Sure I told you that afoul" (515.26). The Wakean witness is reduced to Mister Bones in a minstrel show, and perhaps an ineffectual Stephen Dedalus as well: "You were ever the gentle poet" (515.34), who is directed to begin his next statement with "once upon a grass and a hopping high grass it was" (516.01). Yawn-Shaun-Stephen will adopt a stage Irishman's brogue to tell them nothing: "Faith, then, Meesta Cheeryman, first he come up, a gag as a gig. . . . Then, begor, counting as many as eleven to thirtytwo seconds with his pocket browning, like I said, wann swanns wann, this is my awethorrorty, he kept forecursing hascupth's foul Fanden" (516.03).

Though they had at first adopted a tone of coaxing and cajoling with a seemingly pliant witness, Mamalujo have lost their patience altogether. They are fed up with this "cock and a biddy story" (519.08), and they take Yawn-Shaun to task over the inaccuracies and contradictions in what they call his story or history: "This is not guid enough, Mr Brasslattin. Finging and tonging and winging and ponging. And all your rally and ramp and rant! Didget think I was asleep at the wheel?" (519.16). Bringing to bear another of his clever tactics, Yawn-Shaun ducks out of the conflict by appealing to Johnny MacDougall, a strategy of divide and conquer. It is not his fault if the facts will not fit together, since all the information he has offered was picked up in conversations with Luke Tarpey and the other two historians Lyons and Gregory. He says, "It was told me as an inspired statement by a friend of myself, in reply to salute, Tarpey, after three o'clock mass" (519.30), and he goes on to incriminate Tarpey's cronies.

Yawn-Shaun's ploy is successful, and Johnny's indignation is matched by Matt's angry retort that Johnny must have been bribed with drink to entertain such a ridiculous idea: "Come now, Johnny! We weren't born yesterday. . . . I ask you to say on your scotty pictail you were promised fines times with some staggerjuice or dead horse, on strip or in larges, at the Raven and Sugarloaf, either Jones's lame or Jamesy's gait, anyhow?" (521.10). As this section comes to a close, Yawn-Shaun is momentarily safe from questions. After an exchange of insults, the three gang up on Matt Gregory. They say, "Guid. We make fight! Three to one! Raddy?" (521.31), and the poor scholar from Ulster is forced to run for his life. Again, shillelagh law is all the rage.

Yawn-Shaun will be placed in the spotlight a third and final time, but the clarity, if one may call it that, of the previous sections is not to continue. The unity or the identity of the voice emanating from the speaker will be fractured, as Yawn-Shaun gives up hope of ever inducing Mamalujo to understand. He will willingly give up his control to any other voice which is inclined to take over the frequency. The Four are aware by this time that the nature of Earwicker's Sin is clouded in multiplicity: "There are sordidly tales within tales, you clearly understand that?" (522.05), they say, but their guesses are trailing off into the ridiculous and the nonsensical. "Which moral turpitude would you select of the two, for choice, if you had your way? Playing bull before shebears or the hindlegs off a clotheshorse?" (522.14). The impatient answer, "Buggered if I know!" (522.18) mirrors the irritation of Yawn-Shaun and the reader, and it signals the moment of Yawn-Shaun's disappearance.

Once again the pattern is one of a movement from seeming organization to disintegration. With the warning that he will no longer be responsible for anything which is said—"Are you to have all the pleasure quizzing on me? I didn't say it aloud, sir. I have something inside of me talking to myself" (522.25)—he rejects their implying that he is mad and in need of treatment: "I can psoakoonaloose myself any time I want (the fog follow you all!) without your interferences or any other pigeonstealer" (522.34). And lose himself he does indeed, retreating behind the curtain while other voices offer their own opinions and suppositions.

After a cameo appearance by Issy, who seems to think that she is being interviewed by a newspaper reporter—"has it become to dawn in you yet that the deponent, the man from Saint Yves, may have been (one is reluctant to use the passive voice) may be been as much sinned against as sinning" (523.07)—we get a general delivery of yesterday's news from a representative of the Twelve, who says, "Pro general continuation and in particular explication to your singular interrogation our asseveralation" (523.21). This personage turns out to be Treacle Tom, making the rounds of the pubs with his pal Frisky Shorty, and "having a wee chatty with our hosty in his comfy estably over the old middlesex party and his moral turps" (523.26). His solution to the Earwicker problem is a prescription for cold showers regularly, and a newly written or discovered stanza of "The Ballad of Persse O'Reilly" now names the dastardly culprit as "our Human Conger Eel!" (525.26).

The reference to HCE as a sea creature reawakens Mamalujo's interest and recalls their self-designation as fishermen casting nets, leading on to their remembering the accents of the two washerwomen and the conversation across the Liffey River: "Among the shivering sedges so? Weedy waving. . . . —Besides the bubblye waters of, babblyebubblye waters of?" (526.05). Things simply will not hold together, and each new speaker takes the focus of the testimony farther afield. A Mamalujo comment that they seem to have overlooked the perspective of the women in this case—"You're forgetting the jinnyjos for the fayboys" (526.17)—brings on Issy, who does not even realize that she is being interrogated. Instead of acknowledging her audience, Issy, like Esther Summerson again, holds a conversation with her doll or her mirror personality: "It's meemly us two, meme idoll" (527.24), and she warns against having anything to do with these strange goings on: "Of course I know you are a viry vikid girl to go in the dreemplace and at that time of the draym and it was a very wrong thing to do, even under the dark flush of night" (527.05).

To conclude her appearance here, Issy's voice is gradually fading away, like Margareena in the tale of Burrus and Caseous: "I'm fading. . . . I'm fay" (528.11). As usual, Mamalujo are unable to grasp what is going on: "How is this at all. Is dads the thing in such or are tits the that? . . . Is she having an ambidual act herself in apparition with herself as Consuelas to Sonias may?" (528.15). All the possible sources of information are drying up, and Luke, for a moment sounding like Simon Dedalus making fun of the pronunciation of the Goulding family,[5] attacks Mark and demands his fair share of the airtime: "Dis and dat and dese and dose! Your crackling out of your turn, my Moonster firefly, like always . . . stay off my air! . . . my queskins first, foxyjack!" (528.26). In desperation, they call for the Earwicker servants, but Sackerson or Joe makes no sense, and Kate the Slops will only complain about interference in her kitchen: "For the loaf of Obadiah, take your pastryart's noas out of me flouer bouckuet!" (531.11). The disconnectedness of these answers has finally begun to wear down the Four. This is getting everybody nowhere, since there is no telling who will speak next or what he or she might say in yet another digression. It is time to stop, to reconsider, and to look at one last witness: "All halt! Sponsor programme and close down. That's enough, genral, of finicking about Finnegan and fiddling with his faddles" (531.27).

Now that all of the other personages have left the line, there is only one voice left to contact, HCE himself, who now will be given as much room as he needs to defend and explain his position. With the invocation "Ho, croak, evildoer! Arise, sir ghostus! As long as you've lived there'll be no other. Doff!" (532.03), Earwicker speaks and will dominate the rest of the chapter. But, as was stated earlier, the Mamalujo method of question and answer will not solve the nightmare of history. Earwicker knows how to manipulate an audience, and, after asserting the solidity of his public reputation— "I think how our public at large appreciates it most highly from me that I am as cleanliving as could be" (532.16)—he deflects attention away from himself to side issues like the tiny size of Anna Livia's charming feet. "She is my bestpreserved wholewife, sowell her as herafter, in Evans's eye, with incompatibly the smallest shoenumber outside chinatins. They are jolly dainty, spekin tluly" (533.04).

The onrushing mass of verbiage is proving to be too much for the Four, and they are losing interest and coherence quickly. Where earlier they could maintain control of the inquisition, and bring a speaker back to the subject with a stern and pointed question, now they are lapsing into a babble of their own: "Tiktak. Tikkak. / — Awind abuzz awater falling. / —Poor a cowe his jew placator. / — It's the damp damp damp" (534.03).

Proceeding along again, now as Big Calm, Earwicker will dismiss the Cad as nothing more than a strangler of green parrots, the latter already suffocated to begin with, but even this nonsense cannot rouse the Four to consciousness: "Is that yu, Whitehed? / —

Have you headnoise now? / —Give us your mespilt reception, will yous? / —Pass the fish for Christ's sake!" (535.22). The fish they wished initially to bring up on charges now looks better as simple succor for their stomachs.

Just as it proved virtually impossible to delineate a single person-age standing behind the Yawn voice, so too Earwicker presents a multitude of faces to meet the faces that he meets. First as Big Calm, then Whitehead, then Whitehowth, he metamorphoses into Haveth Childers Everywhere, begging for pity and understanding like Oscar Wilde: "Tell the woyld I have lived true thousands hells. Pity, please, lady, for poor O. W. in this profundest snobbing I have caught" (535.27). Leaping nimbly from one rhetorical posi-tion to another, he declares his openness and honesty: "Well, yeamen, I have bared my whole past, I flatter myself, on both sides" (536.28). He denies any association whatsoever with the girls in the Park: "I their covin guardient, I would not know to contact such gretched youngsteys" (538.23).

It is not clear what has happened to Mamalujo, where they are or whether they are listening at all, since page after page of the monologue flows along without any outside interruption. Earlier in this chapter, they would leap upon any suspicion of a double entendre lurking in the language that they heard, but now they allow Earwicker to get away with almost anything, as he continues to "testify to my unclothed virute by the longstone erectheion of our allfirst manhere. I should tell you that honestly, on my honour of a Nearwicked" (539.02). Moving easily from one erection to another, he says that not only has he run his pub successfully, but he has also participated in the raising of many of the buildings in the town. Switching the subject from himself again to the beauty of Dublin and environs, HCE sounds as much like a member of the Chamber of Commerce as he does like Holinshed: "This seat of our city it is of all sides pleasant, comfortable and wholesome. If you would traverse hills, they are not far off. If champain land, it lieth of all parts. If you would be delited with fresh water, the famous river, called of Ptolemy the Libnia Labia, runneth fast by. If you will take the view of the sea, it is at hand. Give heed!" (540.03). As the problem of the Sin is pushed into the background, this Earwicker voice becomes more self-assured, loses its stutter and its Freudian slips, and leads Mamalujo gently down the garden path.

The Four's only comment is to cheer him on, as Earwicker grandly proclaims something which sounds suspiciously close to the New Bloomusalem in the Nova Hibernia of the future. Not only does he claim to be a builder—"I raised a dome on the wherewithouts of Michan" (541.05)—he also declares himself a hero for all the ages, more accomplished than Daniel in the lions' den, or Brian Boru, or even the Duke of Wellington. As his speeches rumble along and pick up steam, HCE embarks on a long peroration celebrating his accomplishments and his family history, always insisting upon the propriety of his position in the community: "respected and respectable, as respectable as respectable can respectably be" (545.11). He describes his statement as a "holocryptogam" (546.13), and in many ways this is exactly what it is. It is a document written entirely in his own hand, with a bit of a cryptogram thrown in for self-protection, with an emphasis on the "gam," or the chatty conversation or social visit, which Earwicker is creating now for the reader. Mamalujo's periodic comments indicate that they have long since stopped following the speech: "What is your numb? Bun! / —Who gave you that numb? Poo! / —Have you put in all your sparepennies? I'm listening. Sree! / —Keep clear of propennies! Fore!" (546.25). They seem ready to say farewell once and for all: "Till we meet! / —Ere we part! / —Tollollal! / —This time a hundred years!" (547.10).

Pretty much freed from the Four, Earwicker has really no listener now but the reader, and these closing passages, while they do present the passing out of the father, his decline, are certainly as well a tribute to the nobility of his selfhood. He has not done so badly after all. Looking backward once again, he drops his social accomplishments and celebrates his love for Anna Livia: "for I waged love on her" (547.07). With all guilt gone, he fuses the real and the ideal in his description of their first lovemaking in a way which is as touching as it is forthright. "I abridged with domfine norsemanship till I had done abate her maidan race, my baresark bride, and knew her fleshly when with all my bawdy did I her whorship. . . . And I cast my tenspan joys on her, arsched overtupped, from bank of call to echobank . . . so streng we were in one, malestream in shegulf" (547.26).

In many ways, this must be seen as a substantiation of the validity of their coming together in bed in the next chapter. HCE does not rue the past; he recaptures it triumphantly. With no Mamalujo to snicker, as they did at Tristan and Isolde, he becomes unabashedly romantic and sentimental: "I was her hochsized, her cleavunto, her everest, she was my annie, my lauralad, my pisoved" (548.09). As a result of their union, "what was trembling sod quaked no more, what were frozen loins were stirred and lived" (549.08). Like Bloom with Molly, Earwicker has attempted to improve Anna Livia's mind: "her intellects I charmed with I calle them utile thoughts" (549.30). It becomes clear, however, that intellectual or not, she is the center of his universe.[6] Perhaps it is not too much to say that, left on his own, Earwicker offers the highpoint of *Finnegans Wake,* the rationale of the union of the male and the female which, Joyce seems to imply, makes it all worthwhile. The misguided questioning which has gone before is reduced to nothing by HCE's realization that such celebration of the past is, in turn, a celebration, or at least acceptance, of the present and the future.

Ironically enough, in a chapter in which voice has been stripped to its bare essentials, it is Earwicker who restores life to speech as he acknowledges his debt to Anna Livia. Everything that he has done has been for her. Amid all the preceding chatter, it is his voice which stands out, and even Mamalujo's final comments seem to be more an acclamation than a quibble: "Hoke! / —Hoke! / —Hoke! / —Hoke!" (552.31). On an archetypal level, HCE and ALP are father and mother, a king and a queen, and in a final vision they parade through the streets of Dublin in state. Tellingly, though, the focus remains upon Anna Livia rather than her consort: "Lawdy Dawe a perch behind: the mule and the hinny and the jennet and the mustard nag and piebald shjelties and skewbald awknees steppit lively (lift ye the left and rink ye the right!) for her pleashadure: and she lalaughed in her diddydid domino to the switcheries of the whip" (554.04). All of the supporting cast is gone, and Earwicker can ultimately dismiss Mamalujo and everything they represent. "Down with them! Kick! Playup! / Mattahah! Marahah! Luahah! Joahanahanahana!" (554.09). Exposed and undercut with laughter, the Four are no longer a factor. In accepting the past and embracing it joyfully, Earwicker renders guilt and the Sin irrelevant.

Margot Norris says that "the *Wake* is also about that fear [of death], about the resistance of Wakean figures to change and decline, about their reluctance to recognize their guilt and mortality, and about their escape into the defenses, disguises, illusions, and myths available to them in the dream."[7] I agree. But here, at the end of III.3, HCE looks clearly at himself and at his familial position, and escape no longer seems necessary for him. Certainly nothing is finally resolved, as was the case with Bloom's consternation over Molly's adultery, but at least Earwicker seems to be moving closer to the all-important "equanimity."

While indeed this is not necessarily optimistic, certainly it is affirmative. Leopold Bloom on Sandymount strand was unsure of how to complete "I am a," written with a stick in the sand, but perhaps Humphrey Chimpden Earwicker now can write "I am a Man," and perhaps, at least for him, this is what *Finnegans Wake* is all about.

Afterword: Their Tales within Wheels and Stucks between Spokes

(247.03)

Just as *Ulysses* is neither a demonstration of the squalid reality of Dublin on June 16, 1904, nor a paean of praise for the great healing powers of a fertile earth mother named Molly, so too should we be cautious about extremes when attempting to delineate the thematic concerns of *Finnegans Wake*. The novel is neither a portrait of a sterile and impotent father, nor a glowing tribute to some sort of regenerative river or ocean nymph called Anna Livia. Any and all of these positions are too simplistic to encompass Joyce's fictions. In each of the last two novels, the final appearance of the male is rounded off by the first-person statement of the female, and perhaps the stasis which is achieved at the end of *Ulysses* can serve as a venue into the ultimate significance of *Finnegans Wake*. In the case of Leopold Bloom, both he and we are left with a state of equanimity, and the same feeling should apply to Humphrey Chimpden Earwicker. Certainly there will be another day on June 17, 1904, rife with possibilities for individual action, and certainly the sun will shine once more over Chapelizod, but in a thematic sense this is irrelevant. The readiness will be all. The central focus of the *Wake* is the balance of the male with the female, an archetypal oneness, and this is what seems to have been accomplished with Earwicker and Anna Livia.

To be realistic for a moment, fathers and mothers are not generally overthrown by sons and daughters, no matter how often this critical chestnut has been used to describe the *Wake*. Perhaps, even for Freud, this supplanting of the generations can function as a metaphor for a graceful (it is to be hoped), passing into middle age, something represented by HCE and ALP. Everyone and everything gets older, but Joyce does not necessarily view this as an utter calamity. The important thing is the acceptance of the new role, something that Simon Dedalus, for instance, does not understand in *A Portrait of the Artist*. Despite his assertion of the democratic nature of his relationship with his son—"I'm talking to you as a friend, Stephen. I don't believe in playing the stern father. I don't believe a son should be afraid of his father. No, I treat you as your grandfather treated me when I was a young chap. We were more like brothers than father and son"[1]—his ego refuses to allow Simon to put such an ideal into practice. His vanity and insecurity, mixed with several John Jamesons in a Cork pub, cause a complete turnabout: "There's that son of mine there not half my age and I'm a better man than he is any day of the week. . . . I'll sing a tenor song against him or I'll vault a fivebarred gate against him or I'll run with him after the hounds across the country as I did thirty years ago along with the Kerry Boy and the best man for it."[2]

But the elder Dedalus is not the elder Earwicker, and HCE seems much more at ease with his own position by the time he has gotten to the last three chapters of the novel. Earwicker's thoughts are on his wife and on himself—he is not looking fearfully over his shoulder at his sons—and any conflict seems resolved. The thematic resolution is much less vindictive and melodramatic than the Freudian straining of an interpretation which sees the children as adversaries, victorious "by developing to the point of sexual maturity, at which point the father becomes no father, and a new father is created, with all the fears of the old one haunting him. With the old father out of the way, the new holy marriage between brother and sister can take place (in the archetypal family all sexual relationships are perforce incestuous)."[3] There is little justification for such a position in the text itself.

Vague and fuzzy thinking of this kind has plagued Wakeans for many years, an approach which looks around the novel, rather than within it. There has always been a whatness in the work of James Joyce; he does not write about vague and amorphous shapes which flit in and out of a fictional never-never land. It will not do to say that "the search for the 'facts,' the 'objective' truth, is a red herring that conceals the real issue: the universal guilt resulting from the oedipal relationship to one's parents, the Original Sin descended from Adam and Eve."[4] Such guilt may indeed have been a problem for the little man from Vienna, but it is problematic to assert that this should apply to us all. It would seem to be a fact, though certainly a fictional fact, that Earwicker has not absconded, passed away, or been overthrown in some way or another at the conclusion of *Finnegans Wake*. He is solidly, sleepily, satisfied in bed at the end of IV.1, and that is where we leave him, just as we did Bloom. Even as the novel returns to its starting point, Earwicker will return to a new day. Whether he is better, or sadder or wiser, is moot, but he seems to have assessed this mid-place in his life quite thoroughly, and once again he can willingly carry on.

None of the three Earwicker children seems guilty over some sort of purported sexual relationship with one of the parents, and marriage is certainly not in the picture for Issy, at least not with Shem or with Shaun. It is true that Earwicker notes his daughter's growing maturity, but Anna Livia never even notices anything sexual about the sons. There is indeed a great deal of sexual innuendo throughout the narrative, but the only sexual activity which is described takes place between adults. There is a definite difference between the way sexuality is treated in the *Wake* in the children's context and the way it functions with the grownups.

As was mentioned earlier, the only physical lovemaking which actually takes place in the novel is that between Tristan and Isolde and Earwicker and Anna Livia. With the children, sex is usually treated as a dirty joke, something responded to with a snigger, rather than a lustful sigh. As we have seen, Shaun is the master of the sexual allusion or the double entendre here, sometimes consciously and sometimes not, while Shem is virtually oblivious to the whole thing. Issy looks for the joke or the pun possibility, as she does in the Lessons chapter; responding to Shem's comment that the geometry homework is as plain as day, she says, "as plane as a poke stiff" (296.29), followed by a footnote that shows she is aware of more than a pikestaff: "5The impudence of that in girl's things!" (296.fn.5). But this does not mean that sex is on the minds of the children to any obsessive degree, and they certainly are not very much troubled by it, any more than would be any halfway normal adolescent. The Earwicker siblings can be as ornery and cantankerous, and as mutually understanding, as any ordinary brothers and sisters can be, and we distort the *Wake*'s basic aim of the depiction of a family if we look too hard for the unusual or abnormal sexuality which simply does not appear in the narrative.

As with *Ulysses, Finnegans Wake* is a middle-aged novel, written for a middle-aged reader. It is not concerned with the stirrings of first love but rather with the various aspects of a mature relationship. Erich Fromm notes Ralph Waldo Emerson's statement that "a skillful man reads his dreams for his self-knowledge; yet not the details, but the quality."5 It is not really the details of Earwicker's remembrances which matter so much here, as does the way in which he can finally structure his memories to give them shape and meaning. Too much has been made of the father's sin and his desires to avoid the truth. A reading of *Oliver Twist* will alert us to the fact that "to earwig" is underworld slang for "to confess," but about what does this Joycean father and husband finally admit his guilt? He has not betrayed Anna Livia, nor has he molested his daughter, and, if the incident in Phoenix Park involving the two girls and three soldiers did actually occur at all, it is quite likely that he was simply an innocent bystander as someone urinated in public. This is not an offense which should damn him in the public eye for all eternity. There may be dreams and there may be fantasies, but Earwicker has done nothing which is not understandable and human. As Anna Livia herself is able to sum it up, "All men has done something. Be the time they've come to the weight of old fletch. We'll lave it. So" (621.32).

HCE, like any man, is going the way of all flesh, and whatever may have been done can be just as well either left behind or laved away. Anna Livia does not indicate that she is very much concerned. The initial "all men" of this passage is also the concluding blessing, "amen." The wife provides the final note of healing and encouragement: "It's Phoenix, dear. And the flame is, hear! Let's our joornee saintomichael make it. Since the lausafire has lost and the book of the depth is. Closed. Come! Step out of your shell" (621.01). Like the mythical bird, like the Roc which appeared to Leopold Bloom, the symbol indicates that Earwicker is spiritually rejuvenated. His sojourn in this book is ended, and he can step forward into another morning.

As a final note, it should also be stated that the last few pages of the *Wake* demonstrate a coming together, rather than a sundering. If nothing else, there is fusion and form. To be sure, Anna Livia is more than aware of her husband's foibles and faults, as is Molly Bloom, but there is no reason to take literally ALP's fear that she may soon be replaced by "a daughterwife from the hills again" (627.02). Such behavior would be heavily frowned upon by the Catholic Church in Ireland. Actually, in her dream monologue Anna Livia is becoming that very "daughterwife" herself, as Earwicker metamorphoses in her mind into both father and husband. In what is almost her final statement, this change and fusion becomes clear to the reader. Prefaced and closed by a Molly-like affirmation, Anna Livia transcends age and accepts both roles at once. "Yes. Carry me along, taddy, like you done through the toy fair! If I seen him bearing down on me now under whitespread wings like he'd come from Arkangels, I sink I'd die down over his feet, humbly dumbly, only to washup. Yes" (628.08).

Obviously, there will be no conclusion,[6] as the last page leads back to the first, but some sort of catharsis has been achieved. HCE is the father, and he is also the Humpty Dumpty husband who has been put back together once more. Both Anna Livia and Earwicker have come to a point at which they can look both backwards and forwards at one and the same time: "If I lose my breath for a minute or two don't speak, remember! Once it happened, so it may again" (625.28). Perhaps it is this ability which results in the aforementioned equanimity which ultimately envelopes the characters, and perhaps also, as *Finnegans Wake* comes to a close, a "the" is as good as a "Yes."

Notes

Introduction

1. Stuart Gilbert, ed., *Letters of James Joyce* (New York: Viking Press, 1957), p. 251.

2. Ibid., p. 261.

3. Ibid., p. 220.

4. Ibid., p. 246.

5. See, for example, Derek Attridge and Daniel Ferrer, eds., *Post-structuralist Joyce: Essays from the French* (Cambridge: Cambridge University Press, 1984).

6. Quoted by Erich Fromm, *The Forgotten Language: An Introduction to the Understanding of Dreams, Fairytales, and Myths* (New York: Holt, Rinehart & Winston, 1951), p. 110.

7. Grace Eckley is even more specific than this: "I discovered the original of the character of Humphrey Chimpden Earwicker in William T. Stead, assistant editor in 1885 of *The Pall Mall Gazette*. . . . The Stead history eliminates the mysteries surrounding Earwicker's 'sin.'" *Children's Lore in Finnegans Wake* (Syracuse: Syracuse University Press, 1985), p. xiii.

1—So This is Dyoublong?

1. Quoted in Robert H. Deming, ed. *James Joyce: The Critical Heritage,* vol. 2 (New York: Barnes and Noble, 1970), p. 564.

2. *Further Recollections of James Joyce* (London: Shenval Press, 1955), p. 8.

3. Richard Ellmann, *James Joyce* (New York: Oxford University Press, 1982), p. 712.

4. *The Art of Telling* (Cambridge: Harvard University Press, 1983),

p. 56. See also his *The Sense of an Ending* (New York: Oxford University Press, 1967).

5. *The Art of Telling*, p. 82.

6. *Ulysses* (London: George Allen and Unwin, 1980), p. 81.

7. *Joyce and Aquinas* (New Haven: Yale University Press, 1957), p. 137.

8. Yet this is exactly what John Bishop would have us do. Any section, "like *Finnegans Wake* as a whole, might better be treated as a rebus, a crossword puzzle, or a hardly comprehensible dream whose manifest elements are particles of trivia and nonsense that conceal latent and apocalyptic senses which lie not on the lines but between them" (*Joyce's Book of the Dark: Finnegans Wake* [Madison: University of Wisconsin Press, 1986), p. 315]. For Bishop, the book, which is about the unknowable quality of the night and of dreams, can have no plot and no characterization, and thus no literal meaning. Meaning in the *Wake* is to be arrived at essentially through free association: "Particles of immanent sense will stand out from the dark foil against which they are set, in turn to suggest connections with others, and still others, until—not necessarily in linear order—out of a web of items drawn together by association, a knot of *coherent* nonsense will begin to emerge" (*Joyce's Book of the Dark*, p. 27). Again: "As in a dream, however, this manifest appearance is misleading, since the sense of the dream is latent, buried, and rather than static, charged with a 'constant of fluxion' that makes the release of meaning possible only if one travels along streams of unlimited association" (*Joyce's Book of the Dark*, p. 381).

9. *Further Recollections of James Joyce*, p. 12.

10. Quoted in James S. Atherton, *The Books at the Wake* (New York: Viking Press, 1974), p. 17.

11. *Ulysses*, pp. 61–71. David Hayman first uses the term "arranger" in *Ulysses: The Mechanics of Meaning (Englewood Cliffs, N.J.: Prentice-Hall, 1970), p. 70*.

12. *Joyce's Voices* (Berkeley: University of California Press, 1978).

13. "The Benstock Principle," in *The Seventh of Joyce*, Bernard Benstock, ed. (Bloomington: Indiana University Press, 1982), p. 18.

14. "The Benstock Principle," p. 19.

15. *The Art of Telling*, p. 90.

16. Joseph Campbell and Henry Morton Robinson, *A Skeleton Key to Finnegans Wake* (New York: Harcourt, Brace, 1944), p. 56.

17. William York Tindall, *A Reader's Guide to Finnegans Wake* (New York: Farrar, Straus and Giroux, 1969), p. 57.

18. Adaline Glasheen, *A Third Census of Finnegans Wake* (Berkeley: University of California Press, 1977), p. xxx.

19. Danis Rose and John O'Hanlon, *Understanding Finnegans Wake* (New York: Garland Publishing, 1982), p. 33.

20. For further discussion of the pot and pole, see Marion W. Cumpiano, "The Flowerpot on the Pole: A Motif Approach to *Finnegans Wake*," *JJQ* 21 (Fall 1983): 61–68.

21. Quoted in Deming, p. 738.

2—My Drummers Have Tattled Tall Tales of Me

1. *Letters of James Joyce,* Richard Ellmann, ed., vol. 3 (New York: Viking Press, 1966), p. 364.

2. Clive Hart relates this to the *Dreaming Back* state in Yeats's *A Vision* and says, "Earwicker is dreaming back into his much glorified past, starting with his present deathlike state (403) and working back to his birth" (*Structure and Motif in Finnegans Wake* [Evanston: Northwestern University Press, 1962], p. 92). Barbara DiBernard borrows a phrase from Hugh Kenner's work on *Ulysses* to call this technique "the aesthetic of delay" ("The Technique in *Finnegans Wake,*" *A Companion to Joyce Studies,* Zack Bowen and James F. Carens, eds. [Westport, Conn.: Greenwood Press, 1984], p. 655). Fritz Senn says, "Events and relations arrange themselves for us if we look, or turn back, and this holds good in a much more retrospectacular way than it does in any traditional novel" (*Joyce's Dislocutions: Essays on Reading as Translation* [Baltimore: Johns Hopkins University Press, 1984], p. 85).

3. *Letters of James Joyce,* Stuart Gilbert, ed., p. 406.

4. "At the Margin of Discourse: Footnotes in the Fictional Text," *PMLA* 98, 2 (March 1983), 211.

5. Ibid., 219.

6. Friedrich Nietzsche, *The Joyful Wisdom,* Thomas Common, trans. (New York: Gordon Press, 1974), p. 74. A copy of this translation was included in Joyce's Trieste library.

7. "The Idea of Time in the Works of James Joyce" (*Our Exagmination* [Paris: Shakespeare and Co., 1929], p. 29).

8. "Mr. Joyce's Treatment of Plot," *Our Exagmination,* p. 132.

9. Ibid.

10. John Bishop sees the telescope as an instrument with which HCE may look upon his dream to perceive things not visible in the light of day (*Joyce's Book of the Dark,* pp. 434–35).

11. Jane Lidderdale and Mary Nicholson, *Dear Miss Weaver* (New York: Viking Press, 1970), p. 370.

12. *Letters of James Joyce,* Stuart Gilbert, ed., p. 242.

13. Patrick A. McCarthy calls i-4 a male section and v-8 a female section, but it is difficult to substantiate his claim that Earwicker dies at the end of 4 ("The Structures and Meanings of *Finnegans Wake,*" *A Companion to Joyce Studies,* Zack Bowen and James F. Carens, eds., p. 583).

14. *Structure and Motif in Finnegans Wake,* p. 81.

15. There is an extended discussion of the melding of Joyce and Shem in John Paul Riquelme's chapter on the *Wake,* though Riquelme is occasionally hard to follow (*Teller and Tale in Joyce's Fiction* [Baltimore: Johns Hopkins University Press, 1983], pp. 1–47). Matthew Hodgart seems quite naive to assert that "the basis of the Earwicker and associated plots is simply James Joyce's autobiography in

a disguised form: the book is a confession, like those of St. Augustine and Rousseau, in which the author accuses himself of various crimes or shortcomings—in Joyce's case mainly sexual malpractices which are more probably fantasised than real" (*James Joyce* [London: Routledge and Kegan Paul, 1978], p. 134).

16. *A Skeleton Key to Finnegans Wake* (New York: Harcourt, Brace, 1944), p. 125.

3—*There Are Sordidly Tales within Tales*

1. *Studies in Joyce* (Ann Arbor: UMI Research Press, 1983), p. 43.

2. Vincent Cheng discusses this section and the dramatic metaphor in *Shakespeare and Joyce* (University Park: Pennsylvania State University Press, 1984), pp. 32–53.

3. *Letters of James Joyce,* Stuart Gilbert, ed., p. 295.

4. *The Critical Writings of James Joyce,* Ellsworth Mason and Richard Ellmann, eds. (New York: Viking Press, 1970), pp. 40–42.

5. *Shakespeare and Joyce,* p. 48.

6. For a discussion of the backgrounds to the Mime, see Grace Eckley, *Children's Love in Finnegans Wake,* pp. 130–180.

7. "Dogmad or Dubliboused?" *Joyce's Dislocutions: Essays on Reading as Translation,* John Paul Riquelme, ed., p. 116.

8. *Shakespeare and Company* (New York: Harcourt, Brace, 1959), p. 185.

9. *Teller and Tale in Joyce's Fiction: Oscillating Perspectives,* p. 133.

10. *Lectures on Literature* (New York: Harcourt Brace Jovanovich, 1980), pp. 379–380.

11. *Strong Opinions* (New York: McGraw-Hill, 1981), p. 71.

12. *Letters of James Joyce,* Stuart Gilbert, ed., p. 241.

13. *Myselves When Young* (New York: Oxford University Press, 1970), p. 187.

14. *The Sigla of Finnegans Wake* (Austin: University of Texas Press, 1976).

4—*Thy Oldworld Tales of Homespinning and Derringdo*

1. *The Decentered Universe of Finnegans Wake: A Structuralist Analysis* (Baltimore: Johns Hopkins University Press, 1976), p. 22.

2. *A Third Census of Finnegans Wake* (Berkeley: University of California Press, 1977).

3. Charles Dickens, *Bleak House* (New York: Holt, Rinehart & Winston, 1970), p. 15.

4. See, for example, James S. Atherton, *The Books at the Wake: A Study of*

Literary Allusions in James Joyce's Finnegans Wake (Carbondale: Southern Illinois University Press, 1974). A copy of Sterne was part of Joyce's Trieste library.

5. Laurence Sterne, *The Life and Opinions of Tristram Shandy, Gentleman* (New York: Odyssey Press, 1960), p. 73.

6. "A Warping Process," *Work in Progress: Joyce Centenary Essays,* ed. Richard F. Peterson, Alan M. Cohn, and Edmund L. Epstein (Carbondale: Southern Illinois University Press, 1983), p. 48.

7. Sterne, pp. 36–37.

5—These Tales Which Reliterately Whisked off Our Heart So Narrated by Thou

1. "Afterword: reading *Finnegans Wake,*" *A Starchamber Quiry,* E. L. Epstein, ed., (London: Methuen and Co., 1982), p. 155.

2. See my *Narrator and Character in Finnegans Wake* (Lewisburg: Bucknell University Press, 1975), pp. 15–123.

3. *Joyce's Voices* (Berkeley: University of California Press, 1979), p. 16.

4. James Joyce, *Dubliners* (New York: Modern Library, 1969), p. 62.

5. *Joyce's Voices,* p. 17.

6. Ibid., p. 90.

7. Sheldon Brivic accounts for the many different voices as being parts of one consciousness, as "blending states of the mind of HCE" (*Joyce the Creator* [Madison: University of Wisconsin Press, 1985], p. 52).

8. Padraic and Mary Colum, *Our Friend James Joyce* (Garden City, N.Y.: Doubleday and Co., 1958), p. 185.

9. *Joyce's Voices,* p. 90.

10. *The Decentered Universe of Finnegans Wake,* p. 91.

11. *Joyce Between Freud and Jung* (Port Washington, N.Y.: Kennikat Press, 1980), p. 213.

12. *Teller and Tale in Joyce's Fiction,* p. 8.

13. James Joyce, *A Portrait of the Artist as a Young Man* (New York: Viking Press, 1960), p. 36.

14. *Dubliners,* p. 29.

15. Ibid., p. 31.

16. Ibid., p. 40. I seem to recall that this was first pointed out to me by Fritz Senn.

6—They Are Tales All Tolled

1. Frank Budgen, *James Joyce and the Making of Ulysses* (Bloomington: Indiana University Press, 1967), p. 105.

2. Roland McHugh, *Annotations to Finnegans Wake* (Baltimore: Johns Hopkins University Press, 1980), p. 474.

3. As Roland McHugh describes it, "It is almost wholly direct speech, but we are never told who speaks. It is however usually possible to recognize the voices of ✗ questioning ⋀ and his replies, but at a later stage other voices invade the simple alternation and one must dissect with great care" (*The Sigla of Finnegans Wake*, p. 44).

4. *The Decentered Universe of Finnegans Wake: A Structuralist Analysis*, p. 61.

5. See Hugh Staples, "Growing Up Absurd in Dublin," *A Conceptual Guide to Finnegans Wake*, Michael H. Begnal and Fritz Senn, eds. (University Park: Pennsylvania State University Press, 1974), p. 193.

6. It is unclear what Adaline Glasheen means when she says, "I feel sure HCE will never repent, is damned. It is not because he has no sense of sin, no social consciousness, nor because he has raped Nature. He is damned because he is Masterbuilder of this our masculine civilization" (*A Third Census of Finnegans Wake*, p. lxv).

7. *The Decentered Universe of Finnegans Wake: A Structuralist Analysis*, p. 97.

Afterword—Their Tales within Wheels and Stucks between Spokes

1. James Joyce, *A Portrait of the Artist as a Young Man*, p. 91.

2. Ibid., p. 95.

3. Edmund L. Epstein, *The Ordeal of Stephen Dedalus* (Carbondale: Southern Illinois University Press, 1973), p. 15.

4. Margot Norris, *The Decentered Universe of Finnegans Wake: A Structuralist Analysis*, p. 91.

5. *The Forgotten Language: An Introduction to the Understanding of Dreams, Fairytales, and Myths*, p. 142.

6. John Bishop attributes lack of actual closure to the nature of association: "particularly because the sense of this book of the dark lies entangled in a network of free associations, it never ends" (*Joyce's Book of the Dark*, p. 385).

Bibliography

Atherton, James S. *The Books at the Wake: A Study of Literary Allusions in James Joyce's Finnegans Wake*. Carbondale: Southern Illinois University Press, 1974.

Attridge, Derek and Daniel Ferrer, eds. *Post-structuralist Joyce: Essays from the French*. Cambridge: Cambridge University Press, 1984.

Beach, Sylvia. *Shakespeare and Company*. New York: Harcourt, Brace, 1959.

Beckett, Samuel, et al. *Our Exagmination Round His Factification for Incamination of Work in Progress*. Paris: Shakespeare and Company, 1929.

Begnal, Michael H. and Fritz Senn, eds. *A Conceptual Guide to Finnegans Wake*. University Park: Pennsylvania State University Press, 1974.

Begnal, Michael H. *Narrator and Character in Finnegans Wake*. Lewisburg: Bucknell University Press, 1975.

Benstock, Bernard, ed. *The Seventh of Joyce*. Bloomington: Indiana University Press, 1982.

Bishop, John. *Joyce's Book of the Dark: Finnegans Wake*. Madison: University of Wisconsin Press, 1986.

Benstock, Shari. "At the Margin of Discourse: Footnotes in the Fictional Text," *PMLA* 98, 2 (March 1983), 209–22.

Bowen, Zack and James F. Carens, eds. *A Companion to Joyce Studies*. Westport, Conn.: Greenwood Press, 1984.

Brivic, Sheldon. *Joyce Between Freud and Jung*. Port Washington, N.Y.: Kennikat Press, 1980.

———. *Joyce the Creator*. Madison: University of Wisconsin Press, 1985.

Budgen, Frank. *Further Recollections of James Joyce*. London: The Shenval Press, 1955.

121

————. *James Joyce and the Making of Ulysses*. Bloomington: Indiana University Press, 1967.

————. *Myselves When Young*. New York: Oxford University Press, 1970.

Campbell, Joseph and Henry Morton Robinson. *A Skeleton Key to Finnegans Wake*. New York: Random House, 1944.

Cheng, Vincent. *Shakespeare and Joyce*. University Park: Pennsylvania State University Press, 1984.

Colum, Mary and Padraic. *Our Friend James Joyce*. Garden City, N.Y.: Doubleday and Company, 1958.

Cumpiano, Marion W. "The Flowerpot on the Pole: A Motif Approach to *Finnegans Wake*," *JJQ*, 21 (Fall 1983), 61–68.

Deming, Robert H., ed. *James Joyce: The Critical Heritage*. 2 vols. New York: Barnes and Noble, 1970.

Dickens, Charles. *Bleak House*. New York: Holt, Rinehart & Winston, 1970.

Eco, Umberto. *The Aesthetics of Chaosmos: The Middle Ages of James Joyce*. Tulsa: University of Tulsa Press, 1982.

Eckley, Grace. *Children's Lore in Finnegans Wake*. Syracuse: Syracuse University Press, 1985.

Ellmann, Richard. *The Consciousness of Joyce*. New York: Oxford University Press, 1981.

————. *James Joyce*. New York: Oxford University Press, 1982.

————, ed. *Letters of James Joyce*. 2 vols. New York: Viking Press, 1966.

Epstein, Edmund L. *The Ordeal of Stephen Dedalus*. Carbondale: Southern Illinois University Press, 1973.

————, ed. *A Starchamber Quiry*. London: Methuen and Company, 1982.

Fromm, Erich. *The Forgotten Language: An Introduction to the Understanding of Dreams, Fairytales, and Myths*. New York: Holt, Rinehart & Winston, 1951.

Gilbert, Stuart, ed. *Letters of James Joyce*. New York: Viking Press, 1957.

Glasheen, Adaline. *A Third Census of Finnegans Wake*. Berkeley: University of California Press, 1977.

Halper, Nathan. *Studies in Joyce*. Ann Arbor: UMI Research Press, 1983.

Hart, Clive. *Structure and Motif in Finnegans Wake*. Evanston: Northwestern University Press, 1962.

Hayman, David. *Ulysses: The Mechanics of Meaning*. Englewood Cliffs, N.J.: Prentice-Hall, 1970.

Hodgart, Matthew. *James Joyce*. London: Routledge and Kegan Paul, 1978.

Joyce, James. *Dubliners*. New York: Modern Library, 1969.

———. *A Portrait of the Artist as a Young Man*. New York: Viking Press, 1960.

———. *Ulysses*. New York: Random House, 1986.

———. *Finnegans Wake*. New York: Viking Press, 1964.

Kermode, Frank. *The Art of Telling*. Cambridge: Harvard University Press, 1983.

———. *The Sense of an Ending*. New York: Oxford University Press, 1967.

Kenner, Hugh. *Joyce's Voices*. Berkeley: University of California Press, 1979.

———. *Ulysses*. London: George Allen and Unwin, 1980.

Lidderdale, Jane and Mary Nicholson. *Dear Miss Weaver*. New York: Viking Press, 1970.

McHugh, Roland. *Annotations to Finnegans Wake*. Baltimore: Johns Hopkins University Press, 1980.

———. *The Sigla of Finnegans Wake*. Austin: University of Texas Press, 1976.

Mason, Ellsworth and Richard Ellmann, eds. *The Critical Writings of James Joyce*. New York: Viking Press, 1970.

Nabokov, Vladimir. *Lectures on Literature*. New York: Harcourt Brace Jovanovitch, 1980.

Nabokov, Vladimir. *Strong Opinions*. New York: McGraw-Hill, 1981.

Nietzsche, Friedrich. *The Joyful Wisdom*, Thomas Common, trans. New York: Gordon Press, 1974.

Noon, William T. *Joyce and Aquinas*. New Haven: Yale University Press, 1957.

Norris, Margot. *The Decentered Universe of Finnegans Wake: A Structuralist Analysis*. Baltimore: Johns Hopkins University Press, 1976.

Peterson, Richard F., Alan M. Cohn, and Edmund L. Epstein, eds. *Work in Progress: Joyce Centenary Essays*. Carbondale: Southern Illinois University Press, 1983.

Riquelme, John Paul. *Teller and Tale in Joyce's Fiction: Oscillating Perspectives*. Baltimore: Johns Hopkins University Press, 1983.

Rose, Danis and John O'Hanlon. *Understanding Finnegans Wake*. New York: Garland Publishing, 1982.

Senn, Fritz. *Joyce's Dislocutions: Essays on Reading as Translation*. Baltimore: Johns Hopkins University Press, 1984.

Solomon, Margaret. *Eternal Geomater: The Sexual Universe of Finnegans Wake*. Carbondale: Southern Illinois University Press, 1969.

Sterne, Laurence. *The Life and Opinions of Tristram Shandy, Gentleman*. New York: Odyssey Press, 1960.

Tindall, William York. *A Reader's Guide to Finnegans Wake*. New York: Farrar, Straus, and Giroux, 1969.

Index

125

DREAMSCHEME
was composed in 10 on 12 Galliard on a Mergenthaler Linotron 202
by Coghill Book Typesetting Co.;
with initial capitals in Celtic Alphabet provided by Jōb Litho Services;
printed by sheet-fed offset on 60-pound, acid-free Glaffelter Natural Hi Bulk,
Smyth sewn and bound over binder's boards in Holliston Roxite C,
by Braun-Brumfield, Inc.;
with dust jackets printed in 2 colors by Braun-Brumfield, Inc.;
designed by Vicky Welch;
and published by
SYRACUSE UNIVERSITY PRESS
SYRACUSE, NEW YORK 13244-5160